BLACK BELIEF

Folk Beliefs of Blacks
in America and West Africa

BLACK BELIEF

Folk Beliefs of Blacks in America and West Africa

Henry H. Mitchell

HARPER & ROW, PUBLISHERS

New York   Evanston   San Francisco   London

BLACK BELIEF: Folk Beliefs of Blacks in America and West Africa. Copyright © 1975 by Henry H. Mitchell. All rights reserved. Printed in the United States of America. No part of this book may be used or reproduced in any manner whatsoever without written permission except in the case of brief quotations embodied in critical articles and reviews. For information address Harper & Row, Publishers, Inc., 10 East 53rd Street, New York, N.Y. 10022. Published simultaneously in Canada by Fitzhenry & Whiteside Limited, Toronto.

FIRST EDITION

Designed by C. Linda Dingler

Library of Congress Cataloging in Publication Data

Mitchell, Henry H
  Black belief.

  Bibliography: p. 164
  Includes index.
  1. Negroes—Religion. I. Title.
BR563.N4M57   299'.6   74–4632
ISBN 0–06–065762–6

In loyal and loving memory
of

Martin Luther King, Jr.
(1929–1968)

Whose ministry remains a model
of the best of Black Belief

and

"Hank"
Henry Heywood Mitchell, Jr.
(1945–1972)

Whose devotion and integrity
continue to inspire his Dad.

CONTENTS

ACKNOWLEDGMENTS

No book is written in a vacuum. I am deeply indebted to many. Colgate Rochester Divinity School/Bexley Hall/Crozer Theological Seminary made possible, after urging by their Black Caucus, the years of teaching which stimulated the writing of the seminal lectures which yielded the basic thesis of this work. The seminary's Martin Luther King Program of Black Church Studies' Bibliographic and Curriculum Project made an incalculable contribution to my growth by providing in-depth dialogue with writing-Fellows/Practitioners in Black Religion, as well as enabling me to study further in West Africa and the Caribbean. This MLK Project was funded, in turn, by the Irwin-Sweeney-Miller Foundation, which also provided invaluable guidance throughout the three-year period. The project's African Director, Kofi Asare Opoku was especially helpful.

The Phelps-Stokes Fund offered crucial insights by means of experiences in East African life and culture. And Dorothy Andrews of Altadena gave strategic service at the typewriter.

My deepest gratitude goes to my wife, Ella, whose support of my endeavor spanned the gamut. She scanned thousands of pages, all the while nursing me on my "sick leave" which was spent at the School of Theology at Claremont (California), where I was also Scholar-in-Residence. In its early stages this work served as my Th. D. dissertation there. The administration and faculty were creative in undergirding my efforts, and to them and indeed to all concerned I am most grateful.

HENRY H. MITCHELL

Foreword

The Black Church Studies Program at Colgate Rochester Divinity School/Bexley Hall/Crozer Theological Seminary was the first such program in the nation to be designed and staffed as a correlative curriculum in a predominately White theological school. In April 1969 Henry H. Mitchell was called to be its first director and Martin Luther King, Jr. Memorial Professor of Black Church Studies. As his successor I have fallen heir to what he and the Black students who worked with him were able to accomplish in those tumultuous days of awakening Black religious consciousness. Unfortunately, only a few people are aware of the monographs, research data, tapes, and other resources amassed at CRDS/BH/CTS in the course of attempting to demarcate and institutionalize Black church studies in that early period from 1968 to 1974.

The present work is, in one sense, the first evidence of what he has been about. Although in an earlier book, *Black Preaching,* he set forth some of the themes more carefully explicated here, this work has a more sculptured theoretical framework and more extensive documentation. Critics will not fail to note the sometimes dangerous and daring steps by which Mitchell makes his way into the tortuous and still largely unexplored jungle of the study of Black folk religion. I, for one, must applaud the effort and admire both the intellectual courage and the vitality of this attempt at a radical Black scholarship. It is almost in the idiom and style of the subject being investigated, and it dares to challenge the widely accepted notion that Black religion is little more than a phenomenon of a culture of poverty and racial discrimination.

For many years African religions have been studied ethnographically, first by European missionary-scholars who had learned the native language, and later by African scholars who themselves went out with tape recorder and notebook to penetrate the curtain of exclusivity and idiosyncrasy that surrounds a people of oral rather than written traditions. The result has been to open up the possibility of an African theology that is something more than a blackenization of the canons of Rome, Geneva, and Canterbury. This is what I take Mitchell to be after in an Afro-American context. Very few attempts have preceded him.

It is not that many of us have not tried to uncover the distinctive lineaments of Black American Christianity. It is rather that almost no one has utilized the most recent research of African scholars on their traditional background, such as the proverbs; nor has anyone combed the slave narratives that Julius Lester, George P. Rawick, Norman Yetman and others have reordered out of the plethora of materials left by the Federal Writers' Project of the Works Progress Administration of 1936-1938. This Henry Mitchell has attempted to do, and in so doing he has swept away the ground cover of as yet a still superficial but highly promising stratum of folk religion that must surely be the crucible of an authentic Black theology.

Mitchell's thesis is that Black religion in America is a translation of African beliefs—an adaptation to the needs of the masses and a product of the genius of Black pulpit and people. The manner in which he develops it complements the more celebrated work being done today by the systematic theologians and philosophers of religion. Some will doubtless argue with his evaluation of "high" and "low" religion and his sharp differentiation between "folk terms" and "theological terms." But with ten years in the pastorate and fourteen years as a worker among Black Baptist churches in Northern California, he has a keen ear for the accents of theological discourse that make contact with the people in the pews.

Dr. Mitchell has done a service for Black scholarship in religion. He brings, nevertheless, a parish-oriented and pastoral perspective that will be more helpful to ministerial students and pastors than academicians. For my part, this is a welcome contribution to the development of Black theology these days. It is certain that nothing will prematurely foreclose this movement more quickly than to be perfectly compatible with the professors and perfectly incompatible with a growing group of young laity who want to know what they may confess before God and declare to their children about Black identity, Africa, and our liberation from White religious encapsulation.

GAYRAUD S. WILMORE

ROCHESTER, NEW YORK

BLACK BELIEF

*Folk Beliefs of Blacks
in America and West Africa*

Introduction

It has long been assumed that the enslaved African captives and their American-born descendants were stripped of their original culture, especially of such intangible aspects as world view and value systems. That the effort was made there can be no doubt. That it failed is now equally doubtless. To me the evidence gathered in the course of research is so conclusive that I wonder how we missed it for so long. I say "we" because I was among those once guilty of the pervasive and erroneous assumption of the erasure of the substance of traditional African faith. I am now convinced that the slaveocracy failed to erase African culture, but slowly succeeded in getting Blacks to be ashamed of it. The result was that even though we Blacks continued to use and adapt our heritage, we eventually dropped many aspects of it. In time what our ancestors knew to be African and "proper" was viewed as African and "pagan" or "ignorant." After that it was seen as just "Black" and "undesirable" with consequent psychological damages to Black self-esteem.

The call to write about the roots of Black belief was received and accepted when I saw how much intellectual stimulation and psychic healing came to Black undergraduates, along with the religious insights, during a course in the history of Black religion, with its reappraisal of our often discarded cultural and religious roots. The students did not rush headlong back into the Black church as such, but some achieved an inward peace and self-respect born out of the filling of a vacuum at the center of their being. A careful and comprehensive exposition of what they had responded to with such positive effect had to be written.

Black religion in America is a multifaceted phenomenon, to which more and more people are addressing great and detailed study. In a sense, it constitutes one of the most significant unexplored frontiers of academia. It is the modern counterpart of the gold-laden creeks of mid-nineteenth century California. Not only is it rich and promising; it has its parallel in the kinds of people attracted to the yield. Most of them are, like the White "forty-niner," foreigners and opportunists with no equity or birthright in the holdings. In other words the avalanche of written material on Black culture and religion is all too often the product of shallow research by people from *outside* the Black experience. Even the editors of the really valuable reprints of older Black works often turn out to be alien to the culture.

The fact that the Black style is brilliantly oral, as opposed to print-oriented, only adds to the problem. The Blackamerican community seems, for the most part, unaware of what is happening to the gold-bearing cultural stream which it takes so much for granted. The aim of this work, as of other recent attempts *by Blacks,* is to provide a flow of material on Black religion from a contemporary perspective, as well as from the inside. This is all the more necessary since a great many of the available works, even those by Blacks, predate the emergence of Black Power and its increasing triumph over the subtleties of self-hatred resulting from a White frame of reference.

A second aim of this work is to fill a gap in the recent material. There has been considerable work done to present a Black belief system of liberation constructed largely in the present and addressed to the future. Almost nothing has been done to trace and explicate the historic beliefs which brought "Aunt Jane" and all of us "safe thus far," or at least surviving. My own words leaped at me from a page of Gayraud Wilmore's *Black Religion and*

Black Radicalism: "So must the Black hermeneutic seek to look into the message of the Black past and see what the Black Fathers (*religious* Fathers by my previous definition) could be saying to Black people today."[1] Wilmore quite pointedly suggested that while I had mentioned an important task, I had by no means accomplished it.

The clear need exists, then, for a fresh appraisal of Black religion at the grass roots. Such a work requires the experienced insights of a deeply involved pastor or lay person, as opposed to an exclusively academic professional in one of the time-honored theological disciplines. If the writer is rooted in and legitimately identified with both Black religion in its mass manifestations and with academia, then so much the better. However, my primary function in this effort is not as seminary professor but as veteran practitioner from within Black religion and the Black church. This work draws on thirty years as preacher, pastor, administrator, and community servant, as well as a few years as professor. It also draws from the oral tradition and collected written materials of a family whose "root gran'-pappy" was one of the leaders of the Black church before the turn of the century. My grandfather was one of the Black fathers of whom we speak. But this type of family source is not mentioned to avoid the obligation to be informed by the latest and best of Black thought and perspective. This inside view, therefore, will be governed by the most serious intellectual discipline.

A third need of which I am conscious as I write is at the level of resource materials for the large number of college classes in Black religion. As one who is sometimes asked to do a lecture on the subject in the midst of a course on the same, I find these courses frequently taught by non-Blacks, and even more often taught with bibliographies chosen with little or no discrimination. Even when I have taught my own seminary-level courses on the history of Black religion, I have not been able to suggest what was really needed by way of objective and fair (as opposed to bitterly critical) books on the subject.

Related to the need for at least "equal time" against the hostile and, I feel, inaccurate commentaries on the Black religion of the masses, is a need to upgrade historical and theological insights into the Black religious tradition. Too many who are young, gifted, and Black have never heard more than their home church's unfortunately third-grade theological formulations. Guided by their own best Black and biblical insights, Black thinkers must be helped to find the subtle, hidden strengths which are behind the seemingly repulsive, puritanical, and obscurantist exteriors of the folk belief of the Black masses. Just as it is damaging for public schools to teach children that their parents speak a terribly "improper" language, so also is it psychically undermining to be led to believe that what governed the very existence of one's parents, and sustained them, was a cruel fiction and/or an ignorant cult. The most antiecclesiastical and ultraintellectual Black militant must be given a way of seeing the power and truth in the Black religious tradition. Both for the purposes of personal integrity and Black unity, he must at least find a basis for respecting if not embracing Black religion.

In the attempt to deal with the topic of African and Black-american belief and their relationship, several assumptions have governed the writing, and must be accepted by the reader. The first is that this tradition cannot be interpreted from an agnostic or cynical frame of reference. No matter how Black the interpreter/critic, he can no more do justice to the subject from a stance hostile to religion than he can from similarly exterior White-intellectual perspectives. This appraisal has to be free of foreign criteria, and defined, as *all* Black experience must be defined, *from within.* It is ironical that many Blacks who embrace Black jazz and blues traditions, uncritically and with great joy and psychic healing, find it hard to approximate this cultural self-esteem in relation to the mother of these traditions—Black religion. It seems as if "sophisticated" Blacks are waiting for a final White acceptance of Black religion, comparable to the White embrace and imitation of jazz and blues. Somehow, all too many Blacks seek White "respectability" in, of all places, the point of Black culture's greatest strength. Thus, if a Black religious trait doesn't fit the criteria learned in White-culture education, it is considered useless and counterproductive. It is vitally important to understand and to be on guard against this error. Neither militance nor supposed intelligence can substitute for a sound, inside understanding of Black world view and value systems.

Another assumption has to do with the potential scope of the task, as opposed to the limitations of this work. The task could easily require years and years of careful research and rethinking. But there simply is not time for such deliberation. Carefully weighing the hazards and risks, I have done what many Blacks must do. That is at very least to circulate some hypotheses which are consistent with newer and profoundly more healthy views of Black religion and of all Black culture and life.

Therefore, if this treatment seems to some to be premature and in need of further validation, three subsidiary angles of vision are appropriate in response: (1) The view advanced here is at least as well documented, objectively speaking, as the well-circulated negative view of Black religious tradition. It is far *more* valid if one agrees that every religion and culture has the right and indeed the obligation to evaluate itself according to its own goals and criteria. (2) The prevalence of tradition, as opposed to written data, in oral cultures requires a serious review of what in fact constitutes scholarship. The Afro-American tradition is quite pragmatic and demands the use of scientific methods, but they must be patterned after such a model as that employed in biblical scholarship, which accepts the now-printed oral tradition of the Bible as a given. (3) To the extent that some of what I have to say is based on a necessarily hypothesized continuum of folk tradition, it is far better to circulate it and let it precipitate its own response among Black scholars. This is preferable to letting much that is in print about Black religion roam academia unchallenged. By default, the more negative views, actually *more* hypothetical, have until recently been the most readily available. *Black Belief* is one more entry in the contemporary effort to gain at least "equal time" in the discussions of Black religion.

The kind of scholarship advocated here is aimed at stimulating rather than stymieing further research and response, while offering directions which transcend the limitations of the traditionally held views of Black belief. There is certainly one very convincing model for this, in the person of W. E. B. DuBois. One has only to look at his statements on this African-American continuum in such works as *The Souls of Black Folk* (1903), *The Negro Church* (1903), and *The Negro* (1915). From the latter is taken the following quotation:

> At first sight it would seem that slavery completely destroyed every vestige of spontaneous movement among Negroes. This is not strictly true. The vast power of the priest in the African state is well known; his realm alone—the province of religion and medicine—remained largely unaffected by the plantation system. The Negro priest, therefore, early became an important figure on the plantation and found his function as the interpreter of the supernatural, the comforter of the sorrowing, and as the one who expressed, rudely but picturesquely, the longing and disappointment and resentment of a stolen people. From such beginnings arose and spread with marvelous rapidity the Negro church, the first distinctively Negro American social institution. It was not at first by any means a Christian church, but a mere adaptation of those rites of fetish which in America is termed obe worship, or "voodooism." Association and missionary effort soon gave these rites a veneer of Christianity and gradually, after two centuries, the church became Christian, with a simple Calvinistic creed, but with many of the old customs still clinging to the services. It is this historic fact, that the Negro church of today bases itself upon the sole surviving social institution of the African fatherland, that accounts for its extraordinary growth and vitality.[2]

DuBois was not unaware of his limitations. In his introduction to another book, *The World and Africa*, DuBois frankly stated about that work what would be even more relevant to *The Negro:* "With meagre preparation and all too general background of learning, I have essayed a task, which, to be adequate and complete, should be based upon the research of a lifetime! But I am faced with a dilemma, that either I do this now or leave it to others who have not had the tragedy of life which I have, forcing me to a task."[3]

To which I can say a hearty Amen! One Black historian has remarked, "The man [DuBois] was astoundingly accurate and ahead of his time. We are busy, now, footnoting what he said." I might add that I am footnoting especially what he said about the connection between the African traditional religion of the pre-Christian slave, and the folk Christianity of the later Afro-American slave.

The reader must also assume that this work deals with Black history in search of viable models, inside the culture and already tested, for dealing with the continuing issues of Black existence. The worst of the Black religious tradition has long since been well publicized by folklorists like N. N. Puckett, and by sociologists, anthropologists and historians. Here I seek out relevant information from the most functional and liberating Black religion of the slave and Reconstruction eras. It should be understood that basic Black belief or world view has not changed in any important way since that era. As an insider I offer a view from that perspective which might help to save the Black religious tradition, notwithstanding the fact that other religious traditions are in decline. To do so the *strengths* must be focused on. This will help to overcome the stereotypical escapism and social irrelevance of much of Black-culture religion.

In conclusion, I can only hope that this work will be the beginning of an intensive look at Black folk religion—a first few drops of a flood of insight which will benefit both Black and White. It hardly need be said that I hope it will benefit the great movement of young Blacks to professional training for the ministry. The Rochester, New York, based program of Black Church Studies in which I serve is only one of many with enormously increased seminary enrollments of Blacks. These programs all seek to provide skill and sophistication for the pastoral approach to the hard issues of Black church and community life. At the same time, every effort is made to maintain Black identity, Black cultural habits and "formation," and fluency in the Black idiom. With such tools, the Black ministers and laity of the future will overcome the weaknesses of the Black church developed during the greatly increased oppressions and terrors since 1890. The goal is a return to a relevance seen widely in the Reconstruction Era. Near the conclusion of his recent volume on Black psychology and culture Sterling D. Plumpp sums it all up in some comments on the liberating poetry and other work of Don L. Lee: "But in Black literature Don L. Lee is the most liberating. . . . Don L. Lee is really an old-time preacher using the street symbols, corner raps and the Black Position as his bibles; when he reads his poetry, he preaches, he teaches, he condemns, he lauds, he instills hope, and he warns of damnation. The problem the Black man faces today is for Don L. Lee to get a church and carry on in the tradition of a Bishop (Henry McNeal) Turner."[4]

Plumpp is much more of a Black churchman than a blind and loyal promoter for the present institution as is. But many talented young Blacks are hearing his kind of call. With such an unprecedented supply of leadership that is both charismatically fluent in the culture of Afro-Americans and unequivocally dedicated to their liberation, it is not impossible that we are on the threshold of the most productive period in the history of Black folk religion in America. It is also not unthinkable that some of the crumbs or even the main entree on the rich Black table of tradition might be accepted and used to save the ailing White church. In keeping with an old belief among Blacks, such a new birth of Black-generated warmth, freedom, and ethical relevance could provide one more illustration of the providence of God, well known to work in mysterious ways, long before the Fathers knew of Christ. And, obviously, such a providence would launch a blessing full circle and back to the Blacks, whose deepest concerns could only be advanced by the true salvation of many of America's racial majority. Blacks hold that the greatest sin from which Whites need to be saved is blatant racism, and they welcome all to the blessing of increased ministerial training and Black religious renaissance.

ONE

The Setting

The folk religion of the masses of Blackamericans is clearly an adaptation of the African-traditional-religion base brought over by the various West Africans who were pressed into slavery. Black Religion today is quite properly understood to be profoundly Christian, but it is also still deeply influenced by its African roots. It is far more accurate to speak of Blackamerican Christianity as a point on a continuum beginning in Africa, than to speak of it as the direct descendant of a tradition beginning in Athens or Rome or, for that matter, in England. The European was grafted onto the African, and not vice versa. If one wishes to push the examination of roots all the way back to Palestine, then a whole new set of questions may be raised about the *African* roots and relations of primitive Judaism. Suffice it to say that Blackamerican Christianity as believed and practiced by the masses very definitely is not the long-assumed primary product of White missionary teaching and slavemaster brainwashing.

The evidence to support this position is much more abundant and accessible than has been commonly accepted. While it is true that most scholars, even Blacks, have failed to seek and to take seriously the folk world view or religious beliefs of either Africans or Blackamericans, works which trace other aspects of the African-American cultural continuum are rich in significant data. Such works are filled with subtle religious implications so that scholars like Gayraud S. Wilmore have come to suggest that the most important inheritance of Blackamericans from Africa is not musical or rhythmic or related to other aspects of obvious Black style; it is the Black philosophy, or world view and values. John W. Blassingame has summed it up well in his recent work on the slave community.

> The similarities between many European and African cultural elements enabled the slave to continue to engage in many traditional activities or to create a synthesis of European and African cultures. In the process of acculturation the slaves made European forms serve African functions. An example of this is religion. . . . Christian forms were so similar to African religious patterns that it was relatively easy for the early slaves to incorporate them with their traditional practices and beliefs. In America Jehovah replaced Creator, and Jesus, the Holy Ghost, and the Saints replaced the lesser gods. . . . After a few generations the slaves forgot the African deities represented by the Judeo-Christian gods, but in many other facets of their religious services they retained many African elements.[1]

The early slave, then, was not an eager ex-animist without religious belief. Rather, he was in many ways already a "Christian" believer and practitioner. His apparent openness to the Christian faith stemmed from his desire to follow his strong religious bent in a manner both consistent with his heritage and adequately related to the religious processes and practices of his new home. Slaves, not masters, took the initiative to translate their African beliefs into English and into inescapably Christian terms. They also sorted through the Christian Bible and selected the ideas useful to them in the new slave experience. By the time the masters were widely willing to concede souls to slaves, satisfied that the Christian faith could be used to enforce obedience and increase market value, the slaves had long since established their underground version of the true faith; and they were well along in their own "invisible institution," or underground church.

It should long ago have been apparent that the basic tenets of

Blackamerican belief could not possibly have been taught by whip-wielding workers for the "welfare" of Black souls. At the bottom of all African and Blackamerican belief is an unshakable affirmation of the goodness of creation and of human existence, under the rule of a powerful and benevolent Creator. The slaves were, of course, subjected to great cultural shock and suppression, but they weren't crazy enough to accept so ludicrous a set of White religious contradictions. Their well-documented songs and insurrections prove this. Where, then, could they have gotten their highly supportive beliefs in the justice and providence of God save in their traditional African religious views?

The unrecorded first century and a half of Blackamerican belief saw them accept some new ideas alongside these old African fundamentals. They embraced the idea of hell, as a most appropriate place for the perpetrators of slavery. They balanced this new idea with another one called grace, as a proper remedy for their own increasing sense of individual sin, as opposed to their traditional corporate sense of transgression. In their estrangement from power over their own community they embraced the new nearness of their once too-transcendent deity; and they focused their earlier trust in intermediaries in a new and near and likewise-rebuked-and-scorned Jesus, the Mediator in the White-style Trinity. They baptized their highly healing and expressive possession tradition into a sound manifestation of the presence of the now-only-one Holy Ghost or Spirit, third person in the Trinity. But in this unrecorded period and process, *the African slave was the author of the adaptations,* under the guidance of God, as expressed in and through the spiritual and practical instincts with which He endowed Black humanity. The resulting faith has become so deeply imbedded in the unconscious life of Blackamericans that it still will not give way to the onslaughts of modern disbelief and materialistic inhumanity, even among the most antireligious and/or intellectually cynical sons of the Black culture.

Just as Colonel Higginson's regiment of ex-slave volunteers embraced a powerful desire to liberate their slave brethren, even if it required the last drop of their blood, and yet engaged in ring shouts and the possession of the Holy Spirit every night they were not on duty;[2] so, for reasons not always understood by themselves, do Blackamerican believers still sing and shout and get themselves together for their own liberation, whether in or out of an institutional church. In their minds is the profound belief expressed by the ex-slave Jourdan Anderson, when invited by his former master to return after the Civil War: "Surely there will be a day of reckoning for those who defraud the laborer of hire."[3] That belief in the immutable justice of a powerful and gracious God sustains Black people in their oppression even now. It guarantees that life is still good enough to be enjoyed and celebrated enthusiastically, precisely by the persons thought to be at the bottom of the Western world's pile of powers and possessions.

TWO

The African-American Linkage

American Blacks participate in a form of Christianity that was created and developed in the communal life of Blacks as a people. Just as there is no single author or composer of the religious songs we call "Negro spirituals," so is there no single theologian or group of Black theologians responsible for the typical folk beliefs of Blackamericans—their worship, world view, and value system. The professionally educated Black preacher who is really effective among the Black majority will translate his most sophisticated insights into the folk idiom and imagery of their culture, not vice versa. Wherever the Black masses have a choice, they choose their own culture, maintaining their own continuous style in everything from food to faith.

The fact is that there have been no "scholars" of Black religion, per se, until recently, because the beliefs did not originate in academic settings and were not thought to have scholarly significance. Little was written to describe and record the faith of Black folk, and to write it down even now is to run the risk of the new medium creating a new message. Yet a written interpretation of the folk world view can be as useful as a printed edition of a spiritual. After one concedes that to sing a spiritual from a printed sheet is to alter its character as a folk expression, it is still good to have it in print. It is worth spelling out the reasons for taking this risk before we look at the strong continuum of folk belief.

In the first place, it is important to have a written facsimile of the spiritual as an historical record. The religious music of Blacks has long since moved on to emphases other than the Negro spiritual. Without a written attempt to preserve the words and music we might be in danger of losing the entire legacy. In the second place, contemporary Blacks tend to recover the basic meaning and music from that printed page and to use it authentically, yet in their own individual style. Just as the Blackamerican masses blackenize *all* of the music they sing from a printed page, so do they quite accurately *re*blackenize the printed spiritual. The slow, sad cry of some of the spirituals may no longer be popular, but anyone who has lived through the Black experience in America has the background and feelings to present his own moving and genuine rendition.

In this same fashion, the folk beliefs and day-to-day value judgments of Blacks must be committed to writing. In a world where people try to save themselves the mistakes of previous generations by preserving through the printed word the inheritance of their society's collective learning or experience, Blacks must parallel the process. No matter how wed to an oral tradition, we Blacks must write and circulate our findings in our communal life, so that we too maintain a literature. Succeeding generations may reappropriate and interpret it for their own day. The oral traditions of the Old and New Testaments were belatedly written down for the same kinds of reasons. The inescapable errors of such a process are far preferable to the limitations of remaining exclusively oral.

Overgeneralization is another danger in writing about Black faith, for there are many facets and types of Black religion, just as there are many kinds and conditions of Black folks. However, whatever is typically Black about the religion of Afro-Americans will be found in its purest and most intense form among the masses. The oppression that binds Blacks of all classes together is felt most deeply by the mass majority, and the isolation that begets and maintains a separate Black culture and religion is most prevalent among this group. Majority must never be offered as a monolithic description of all Blacks, but the racial ghettoes of Black America are undeniably the best place to study the characteristics of Black religion and culture. Here the roots and rudiments are clearly displayed.

The African influence has been greatest among the masses ever since the first distinctions were made between house and field slaves. It is true that the cultural and religious traditions of all Blacks were fashioned out of Western as well as African raw materials. But the traditions of the masses represent the least diluted essence and survival of the basic African elements on which all Black culture and religion were originally based. The African folk-culture world view was the starting point for *all* of the African-born slaves, and those African beginnings have at least some influence even among the Afro-Americans who for generations have striven to conform to the White middle class.

The first Blacks were landed in 1619, and the Southern denominational moves to "Christianize" them came two hundred years later. By this time the most White Christians could do was superimpose their formality on a faith that maintained its own previous Afro-Christian character underground. Once the Civil War was over, that faith surfaced officially for the first time. The opposition of Whites (and also some Blacks) to the resurgence of "African cult" is evidence enough that the basic religion remained African, although continuously influenced by Western Christianity.

The secret prayer and praise meetings had literally kept enslaved Africans alive by keeping alive the roots of their African experience. After a century and a half, official Black congregations began to emerge (1770s and 1780s), but they had to be acceptable to White churches on the surface, at least, to retain permission to meet. So the real Black religious tradition stayed underground in the South until emancipation came.

This independent Black tradition was aptly termed "the Invisible Institution" by E. Franklin Frazier. It had its own "belief systems, mythologies, symbols and attitudes . . . flowing from the African religious past."[1] And while this theological continuity cannot be so easily documented as can the worship or cultic elements, nevertheless there is massive indirect evidence to balance the dearth of direct documentation of the invisible institution's beliefs.

The matter of records is further complicated. Not only was Black religion underground and out of sight; its practitioners' humanity was not taken seriously. When the records did not even assign names to the slaves, it should surprise no one that they were not expected to have a world view. Therefore, to find Black beliefs, one must obstinately insist upon the humanity and cultural integrity of the enslaved. Then one can find the elusive harder evidence that others have overlooked.

The Visible Continuum

Almost any Blackamerican who today visits the areas of West Africa and the West Indies from or through which the slaves came, will quickly see and feel the truth about the numerous aspects of African culture which have been retained in America.[2] The United States Black will see thousands of West Africans and Black West Indians whose faces seem very familiar, testifying to their common ethnic roots. But much more importantly, the Blackamerican will see kinship in various kinds of behavior as well. A surface sense of being "at home at last" is inescapable for all save the most doctrinaire deniers of the African roots of Blackamerican culture.

For instance, the "returned exile" may never have heard before of a thing called motor inventory, but he will easily see that there are specific muscular movements or ways of using one's body common to Blacks on both sides of the Atlantic. This is apparent in both walking and dancing. The step used in African ceremonial dances, Haitian voodoo rites, West Indian Christian worship, and Blackamerican gospel choirs is strikingly similar. There is even a similarity in the way people hold their mouths when they sing or drum. Herskovits saw it early and clearly, but the fact and/or its significance is still denied by some. DuBois saw the connection even earlier and long before he had visited Africa. His sources, so far as we can tell, were his thorough readings on the subject, coupled with a habit of persistent and perceptive contact with the few African students who came to this country. The vindication of his then-advanced position illustrates the phenomenal powers of a mind open and sensitive to the meaning of Blackness. Today, seventy years after some of his first statements on the subject, the visible evidence of the continuum is predictably less than it was when DuBois first wrote, but it is still sufficient to impress those who are open-minded and aware, and who observe both their American and African kin.

Another surface example is the tradition of having to "dress up" in the extreme for worship, and the worshipful significance that is attached to this.

Although slightly less obvious, the Blackamerican will see the African roots of his instinctive sense of the extended family of "soul brothers." On both sides of the Atlantic, the traditionally intimate community is so deeply imbedded in the Black psyche that it tends to structure all relations. This applies not only to the serious use of titles like brother and sister and mother in a Black ghetto church; it applies to the non–church-related street-culture Blacks in the large cities as well.

In fact, it amazes me that it has often been assumed that these familial titles were, both in and out of religious circles, a vestige of earlier piety. Or, again, titles like uncle and aunt in slave and later Southern culture have been attributed to the White denial of the dignity of Black adults by refusing them the titles Mr. and Mrs. Actually, *inside* the Black community, the wide use of family titles goes back to the African root culture, where everybody "in town" is related by blood. Kinships unto the ninth generation are considered important in many places in Africa. Among the same age set, cousins are literally thought of as brothers and sisters. Blood ties or no, the Black psyche still seeks a community of close kin, in or out of the church.

The most important parallels in style occur in worship. They are apparent to Blacks crossing the ocean either way, when they have no ideological axe to grind and no previous opinions on the subject of cultural survivals. The stateside Black-culture church, storefront or otherwise—Pentecostal, Spiritualist, Methodist, or Baptist—has an unmistakable kinship with African-traditional-religion (ATR) worship.

A Nigerian I met in Ibadan, Western Nigeria, had spent a single year in the United States on a study grant. He frankly admitted that although he had never seriously considered becoming a Christian, he attended a Baptist church in a large Eastern city almost every Sunday. He had even more trouble understanding the English of the Black church than he had had with American English generally, so he understood very little of what was being said, especially at the high moments. But he was deeply at home in the total atmosphere and worship style. It was a taste of home and a psychic healing for a lonesome student. In fact, it was more healing than a typical Christian service in Ibadan, if he had visited a Black congregation of one of the standard American or European denominations. You see, mission churches have tried to suppress the very African culture which the Black-culture churches of America have preserved.

After crossing the Atlantic the other way, a Blackamerican professor had a quite parallel reaction. He was extremely critical of the Black church, while holding a very positive view of African culture, but he freely volunteered that a "fetish sermon" he had heard in Ghana the previous summer was amazingly similar to some sermons he had heard as a boy in a Baptist church in Virginia, near the Carolina line.

Striking similarities between African culture and Blackamerica have a way of popping up most unexpectedly. On a recent trip into East Africa I literally wasn't looking for linkages. American slaves came almost exclusively from the *West* Coast. Imagine my surprise when I heard singing that was so close to the Blackamerican "long meter hymn"* that I instinctively felt I should know the words. I was in, of all places, an Ethiopian Orthodox church in the huge city of Addis Ababa. But the high mass being sung by the priests sounded identical, at times, to the mournful singing of a Black country church, or its storefront urban transplant. Even in West Africa I had heard nothing quite like it.

The modern sociological and anthropological theories about the cultural and religious stripping of the African simply do not explain phenomena like these. Nor do they explain the stability of the Black oral tradition in America, particularly in relation to hymnody.

Worship on the part of the White middle class is oriented to print, and its hymnody has taken several different theological trends in the past century and a half. It was easy to incorporate the ideas of the latest theological fad since new hymnbooks were easily printed and distributed. Old ones were just as easily discarded or given to a poor Black congregation. However, earlier illiteracy among Blacks had caused their hymns to be stored in a more permanent place than a hymnbook. With or without books, many early White hymns were and are still retained and effectively used by Blacks. Black scholars easily assumed this to be worship "dominated" by White culture. What they failed to detect was that the Black means of retention and mode of rendition were the dominant cultural facts. Because most of the music from Africa was lost in the language change, old White hymns have received a Black immortality from slaves forced to sing in English. For example the Black mood and movement of "Amazing Grace" are authentically the slaves' and far removed from the White version of the same hymn. Such is the tenacity and stability of the African root; it can creatively maintain itself by using foreign materials selectively.

*"Long meter hymns" are a Black borrowing and adaptation from early nineteenth-century Protestantism. A leader "lines out" (outlines or preannounces) a phrase or hymn, which is then sung to a standardized chant-tune, with great feeling and slow ("long") pace.

Hard Data Available

Blackamerican Christianity, it is widely believed, acquired its distinctive characteristics from the "African temperament" which had no roots in religious content. That is to say, Black religion brought no ideas from "home." Contemporary Black belief among the masses in America is supposedly compounded of two elements: (a) the Euro-American (White) versions of "Christianity" as taught to slaves and other Blacks in sermons, lessons, hymns; (b) the Black experience, a torture chamber of racial oppression in the United States, lasting more than three centuries, long past the supposed political emancipation ordered in 1865. The theory is deficient, for many reasons, but particularly in that it dogmatically ignores a variety of influences and degrees of influence from the belief systems of West Africa. If one accepts the earlier-mentioned White view of obvious external African survivals, to which Blacks "regressed" after the Civil War, it is easy to see another reason why even Black scholars were anxious to deemphasize African roots. They wanted to claim "good" elements for Black religion and, inescapably, traced them all to Europe and White America. Anxiety to eliminate the "pagan" caused them to disown African content altogether and throw out the baby with the bath.

In 1974 how does one go about tracing these disowned elements from Africa? Scholars readily acknowledge the existence of what Joseph R. Washington, Jr., calls the "African temperament," which he describes as having "remarkable resiliency."[3] What they fail to see is that it must have been based on or contained some sort of world view. African/American-slave capacity to bounce back or to roll with the punches could not have been a mere "primitive" reflex response, devoid of reflection. Such a resilient view need not be established as unique to have been African. Unique or not, its unshakable *affirmation of life*, which carried African people through the hell of slavery, constituted a kind of corporate genius. In degree, if not in kind, it expressed a trust in the goodness of God/reality/life/the-natural-order which was and still is unparalleled. This trustful stance was far more representative of *high religious faith* and of a continuum of African content than any belated belief labels, written in English and "pasted" on the ancient African belief base.

The African world view was not recognized as such because it was so nearly identical with the Judaeo-Christian view, and because it was automatically assumed that religious views as high as this must have come from Whites, not from "pagan" Africans. The speed with which they were "learned" was explained by the assumption that African religious hunger existed in a traditional vacuum. African captives were also assumed to be less rational than Whites, gifted with a simple-minded capacity for blind belief. The overlap between African and Judaeo-Christian oral religious traditions was unthinkable within the biased frame of reference operative among most scholars, Black and White.

The first question likely to be raised in response to the overlap of traditions is, When did Christianity have a chance to penetrate West Africa? One very independent and careful Black scholar shows the belief systems to be historically related, all coming from the prehistoric seat of humanity in East Africa.[4] The Greek roots of Euro-American Christianity are, via Egypt, largely from Africa. The African commonality with Old Testament tradition is well documented, along with the early land bridge between East Africa and Asia Minor. Thus shared prehistoric cultural roots, combined with the shared issues of all human experience, easily explain the similarities between the world view of late-blooming Northern Europe and early-blooming West Africa.

The sustaining power and effectiveness of the Blackamerican adaptation of the West African reading of reality was at work *prior* to evangelization by Whites, and its strength was so great that it has been constantly used and carefully preserved ever since the first gatherings of slaves in the United States managed to communicate with each other. The process was far more folk cultural than consciously intellectual, and often more unconsciously than consciously religious. But it sustained Black survival, and the folks "kept the faith."

No group or race suffering the oppression and brutal treatment heaped on Blackamericans could possibly have remained, for the most part, healthy, sane, and productive without such a strengthening world view as Blacks brought with them from Africa. It was the angle of vision from which all great joys as well as sorrows were seen. For life to continue to be worth living, some sense had to be made of it; some interpretation had to be given to the absurdly cruel and unexplainable experience that they were undergoing. The spirituals are eloquent testimony of how far the slaves were from blissful "ignorance" of the injustices done them. No matter how scientifically naive or politically powerless, *they were aware.* And this awareness would have driven them crazy en masse had they not brought with them a way to view and affirm life when things hit them hardest.

Among the religions and cultures scattered across the face of West Africa this view was relatively similar and still tends to be so. The traditional openness to ideas explains how such religious views were able to spread across West African language and culture lines, even though there was no "missionary" effort to build religious empires. Washington has characterized this easy spread and willing reception of ideas as *open*-mindedness, in contrast with the *empty*-minded interpretations[5] given it by White racists, many of them missionaries. Even today missionaries, some of them Black, misread African open-mindedness as the hunger of religiously "deprived animists." Few seem to understand the African mind as always seeking for something better, to *add* to what he already has, not to replace it. They sought additive improvements among themselves in West Africa, and they sought the same among whomever they encountered in the United States.

The belief system which had spread naturally across West Africa was characterized by a *positive view* of human experience, the spirit world, and the wise and powerful and good God who created the whole business. Few scholars or missionaries ever reported or gave any evidence of understanding this positive view. Stateside Americans as well made the same mistake. They discovered a minority of Blacks who were dominated by the fear of spells and a corruption of original "voodoo," and this was confidently declared to be the fear-ridden Black world view. The perfect stereotype and symbol became a terrified Black with protruding white eyeballs and chattering teeth. With tunnel vision and mixed intent, Whites seldom bothered to take their eyes off the bizarre and look at the vast majority of Blacks who were functioning very courageously in an experience of forced servitude that had killed off or driven crazy most of the White indentured servants and Indian slaves who were subjected to it. Blacks were able to take it not because they were dumb and unaware, as has been stated, but because they had a traditional pattern of trusting God and life and adapting their demands to the limits of reality. Needs which were still unmet, together with final interpretations of human experience, were trusted to the *future* action of a good God, Creator of a benevolent universe. This view was characteristic of virtually all West African traditional religion.

The creative syncretism of the African mentality demanded that every new idea that worked in their hard circumstances be added to their religion. At first the slaves picked up merely bits and snatches of English language and biblical belief. Ultimately they reinterpreted what they had already believed in from the African culture and appropriated enough new insights to be genuinely if not typically Christian. At the same time they remained genuinely though not typically African.

It is easy, and always has been, to trace the increasingly Christian development of Blacks. But the fact was overlooked that they functioned well and increased in numbers of American-born, under the yoke of virtually two centuries of bondage, *before* formal "Christianization." This was accomplished almost exclusively on the basis of their previous world view. Regardless of the records kept by early Whites, and no matter how seldom the Black view was presented to Euro-Americans, the African idea of the universe was in the slaves' mind. Their way of facing tragedy and celebrating life was maintained and fed, as George Rawick suggested, by new arrivals from Africa, for as long as the importation of slaves continued, or nearly two hundred years. It was like the religious revival that comes to the urban ghetto church of the North, out of the waves of migrants from the "purer" springs of Black belief in the rural South. Since Blacks first landed here, however, the African way has been communicated to succeeding generations, as it were, through their mothers' milk, being in the very atmosphere and received both consciously and unconsciously.

The traditional religions of West Africa have changed comparatively little, in their content, in the past half millennium. It is easy to find the *living* remains of our preslavery African forefathers' belief system. On the contemporary end of the time line, where Blacks from the bottom of the socioeconomic heap praise God far more than affluent Whites ever do, it hardly needs to be said that we have evidence of a relatively stable African view. How could we have learned to praise a good God from a White man who usually didn't praise Him himself and who, for generations, had a whip in his hand? We shall deal with this much more extensively later. But it must be said that contemporary praise of God in the ghetto, the perpetually positive reading of reality that allows one to go back "up" when one has been "down," is consistent with and derivative from the like reading of life in the basic traditions of West African religion.

The affirmation typified in the contemporary Black gospel song "God Is So Good To Me," applies to all of God's creations of earth, nature, society, and the individual's personal experience. It constitutes a brilliantly self-fulfilling, accentuate-the-positive life interpretation. It illustrates what the Apostle Paul may have been hinting at when he said that "the just shall live by faith,"[7] but the affirmation in Black world view predates "Christianization" in America, and often exists despite it. This positive view prevailed when a vast majority of slaves were far from formal confessors of Christian faith. It was expressed in praise meetings held at praise houses, full of a real ecstasy over the goodness of God, expressed in songs and dances and shouts.

This positive view came, in fact, from the continent where humanity started, and where the peoples had experienced life and "walked with God" longer than any other race. W. E. B. DuBois quotes Diodorus Siculus as saying:

"The Ethiopians conceive themselves to be of greater antiquity than any other nation; and it is probable that, born under the sun's path, its warmth may have ripened them earlier than other men. They suppose themselves also to be the inventors of divine worship, of festivals, of solemn assemblies, of sacrifices, and every religious practice. They affirm that the Egyptians are one of their colonies."[8]

Neither DuBois nor Siculus likely dreamed that those Ethiopians just might be literally right. How could they know that in October, 1974, anthropologists would find human remains four million years old, suggesting, at least for the time, that mankind started in fact in Ethiopia. Originally DuBois had based his thesis on an old geographical joining of Africa and Asia, at Arabia. This much more recent discovery gives his position a validation by much harder data than he would have dared hope for when he was first advancing his theory. As the ancient quotation implies, the longer human history in Africa, together with a climate less hostile than that in Europe and parts of Asia, would provide a quite understandable basis for the deeply ingrained positive African world view. This view contrasts with the Western, dualistic, acquisitive view of nature and of existence. In the Western view man, the enemy of all things in the natural world, seeks constantly to control and exploit both his environment and his fellow human beings. Even though "sunny" African existence requires hard work and is plagued by such things as tsetse flies, the African had outward as well as inward reasons to be less aggressive and more trustful of the universe and its Creator.

At first glimpse, the miracle is that the positive African view survived at all during the hardships of slavery. It resembles sheer religious genius on a broad racial scale. However, there are some contributing factors. For instance, the long continuous human history on the African continent and the somewhat better climate there gave the ancestors of Africans a kind of unearned head start in their walk with God and their development of a world view.

After Blacks were captured and brought to America, the rules of cultural tenacity applied. Sizable numbers of the enslaved continued to praise God on cultural momentum as well as in quiet desperation. As it turned out, the "praising" served them well, giving them a joyous, celebrative respite from the hardest of human experiences. Their shouting was well recorded by Whites even though Blacks sought to hide it from them. It was also widely referred to in the slaves' own narratives. But ironically, the rationale of all this praising God was ignored, and almost no White recognized it as *high religion*—praise and trust in God, rather than the magic and superstition practiced by some Blacks.

Still another subtle reason for Blacks clinging to their high religion in their low estate was the fact that no other world view, Christian or otherwise, was offered to them on a major scale until they had been here nearly two hundred years. Even then, the Christian view could easily be read to reinforce their African view. There was little or no reason to change, either, because they had found a better way to understand the Christian faith and express it. Now if all this explains away the superior religious genius of Blackamericans, it will at least serve as a resounding refutation of the longstanding caricature of Black religion as ignorant and superstitious.

Ironically, the data gap so apparent in the documentation of high religion (as opposed to charms and spells) during the early slave years is not nearly so applicable to other aspects of Black culture. The hole in the data continuum occurs almost exclusively in world view. The continuum in low religion, magic and superstition, is well established. I shall deal later with the weight and interpretation of this magical continuum. The issue at hand is the odd phenomenon of records kept by Whites that frequently complain about the Blacks' "African" superstition, while at the same time almost completely ignoring their higher insights. Once in a while some saintly Black "Aunty" or "Uncle" is recorded as quoting in the terminology of the Bible her or his early traditional faith erroneously considered to have come from Whites. Otherwise it is understandably difficult to find high religion recorded by those who systematically denied the possibility of its existence among Blacks.

There are facts of Black life in modern America and West Africa that shed light on the processes of the survival of all religion. The related evidence most manifest, of course, concerns low religion—the abundant signs and newspaper ads offering the services of practitioners in roots and charms. Their clients constitute a small minority of Blacks, but their visibility is very high. The purveyors of this magic will vary widely in their ethical sincerity, but all of them represent a corrupt residue of an originally great religious tradition of healing and guidance. Nowhere is this more apparent than in the comparison of the best of Haitian voodoo with what is called by the same name in New Orleans. In assessing the relationship between the two, one can say in one sense that the advertising "root man" constitutes a form of successor to the original African fetish priest of the lesser divinities, or the voodoo *houngan* (priest-doctor). In another sense, the flamboyant "root man" is an unchecked individual entrepreneur of a type almost impossible to find in rural and traditional African society. To the extent that sellers of roots and charms offer the most powerless and frustrated a hope of coping with their problems of love and money and health, they perform a not-always-negative function. On the basis of this they continue to draw some support from those most deprived of other coping options. In the sense that private practitioners have few ties with the Black extended family or its traditional restraints, their sometimes dangerous services represent commerce rather than religion.

Among Blackamerican spiritualist churches or sects, and among many West African cult groups, there is a related magical or low religious approach. Among these cults the extended family pattern prevails, and the possibilities of exploitation are lower. The father-figure/priest may seek to earn his living among the flock, but very few do more than supplement a meager secular income, whether in West Africa or America. Meanwhile, they seek, often quite sincerely, to adapt their original African tradition to modern needs. They may have varying percentages of Christian orthodoxy mixed with varieties of African content. While the West African groups would tend to have greater African content, the American groups would have higher percentages of sheer invention. In both areas, their rating on the scale of low to high religion would vary according to the emphasis on dealing with evil spirits and magic.

The survivals of African low religion are much more obvious than those of the high for at least two reasons. One is that the religion and culture of the power majority engulfed the high survivals. In the United States, "Christianity" selectively absorbed the best of the African religious tradition and then denied its source. In West Africa, the authentic priest of high religion all too often had his privileged constituency siphoned off, except for festivals and dire crises. These lost constituents thought of themselves as crossing over into print and literacy, into the prevailing European language, and into superior medicine, commerce, and status. Meanwhile the traditional priest-doctor was also losing many of his regular adherents to the cities and their various sect substitutes for the family and family-group of the old village. With fewer followers and less financing for their faithfulness, some priests even started their own magical sects. The others became less and less influential.

Another reason for the high visibility of low religion is its higher rate of occurrence, numerically, in nontraditional settings—the high unit count of practitioners' shingles and storefront sect signs in proportion to the low number of persons served. Among their clientele traditional ties are absent, and/or the traditional modes of coping are inadequate to deal with the volume and variety of new problems. Concern for "evil magic,"[9] the hallmark of low religion, increases because of the frustrating failure to meet new needs and the goals introduced by the European power group. To the least learned and most powerless, it is evil magic that is utilized to explain the unaccustomed disintegration in Africa.[10] The process in the United States is closely parallel. In the anxieties of dislocation and change the best and most humane aspects of traditional religion are eroded away. The high, confident vision of God and life is dimmed, along with the warm linkages and effective social controls of traditional society. In almost every case, African high religion winds up stymied and hidden in the White culture confrontation, with Africa maintaining an often only symbolic presence to which all may return on religious feast days, for births, weddings, and funerals, and in other crises.

The less apparent evidence concerning the process of the survival of higher religion lies inside the Black religious tradition itself. It is full of common-sense safeguards against low and/or false religion, and it contradicts the stereotypical view of the Black masses of Africa and America as gullible and even stupid. In response to this inside wisdom, the vast majority of Blackamericans never have deserted the stance of their high and now-biblical tradition. Those who did take the low-religion route usually felt severe stress, and also felt that their higher tradition had failed them in their new and more complicated situations. While the line of demarcation on just how much superstition makes one a low religious would be impossible to draw, there is every appearance that the majority of West Africans in stable communities are just as solidly high religious as the majority of Blackamerican believers.

The oral corpus of African traditional religion is rich in wise counsel on the subject, because the temptation to quick, magical low religion has recurred throughout history, both in and outside the tradition itself. The limitations and failures of witchcraft are proclaimed in numerous proverbs, well known to every traditionally reared West African. They show that low religion is constantly tested pragmatically, and often discarded because it

doesn't work. These proverbs readily explain why magic practice among Africans obtains only among a minority. Here are
some samples, with the emphasis on the "fetish priests" because
they are the closest parallel to the independent root practitioner
and the leader of the small magical sect. I have seen their counterparts in West Africa, with signs placed on streets and road-
sides. I have worked with them in the West Indies. And I have
encountered them by the hundreds in the urban ghettoes of the
United States. To all of these priest-practitioners the African
tradition speaks:

The lazy man failed to find it (i.e. an easy job) and he made for
the house of the Ifa priest (thinking that learning the Ifa oracles
by heart would be easier than working with his hands). (Far
surpassing mere fortune telling, these oracles are very numerous
and sophisticated, demanding staggering memory and very
shrewd insight.) [Yoruba.]

When thirty fetish priests are looking after a sick man, (some
of them) are lying. [Ashanti]

The person who consults it and never dies is not to be found
among the Ifa oracles. [Yoruba]

If a fowl possessed life-giving medicine, would it be taken and
sacrificed over fetishes? [Ashanti]

If the fetish lizard (chameleon) is predestined to be burned, it
will be burned. [Ashanti]

It was a conceited Sigidi who asked to be placed in the rain; as
the arms drop from its body so do the legs; the head alone cannot
stand by itself. (A *Sigidi* is a clay image said to be able to go
secretly at night to wherever its sender wishes in order to harm
someone.) [Yoruba][11]

The fetish priest tells of his victories, but not of his defeats
(that is, boasts of his successful prophecies, but says nothing
about the unfulfilled ones). [Ashanti]

The fetish [really meaning his priest] that is sharp (clever at
predicting events) is the one that has offerings vowed to it.
[Ashanti][12]

The ultimate judgment is reserved for the ultimate crime of

evil magic, as opposed to mere insincerity and fakery. It is exemplified in a Fanti law, typical in West African tradition, which demanded "the death penalty for those found guilty of working evil by the use of magic." Fanti courts still fine or imprison those convicted of using what is referred to legally as "a noxious instrument."[13]

Blackamerican tradition could well use more of this African pragmatism about fetish powers and their results, as well as an ultimate prohibition against the use of evil magic; nonetheless, there are real challenges against unbridled superstition. The lore collected on American voodoo by White folklorists has clearly recorded the close ties with high religion and restraints on evil magic. Puckett includes these statements, even though the major emphasis of his massive work is on evil magic and low religion: "I am informed that Marie Laveau [the oft acknowledged queen of voodoo] was a devout Catholic; she kept a little shrine and . . . had a priest with her just before she died, and even went so far as to conduct the ritual of the original voodoo creed so as to make it conform to the worship of the Virgin and of other saints." He had stated earlier on that "most of the conjure-doctors with whom I have come in contact are unusually religious and ostentatious in their church obligations—some of them even being ministers."[14]

Puckett goes so far as to record that some Blacks believe that "de 'ligion uv de Lawd Jesus Christ will keep off all conjure."[15] Had he looked he would have found a huge majority of this same mind. Rawick's mostly White WPA reporters, who were no less bent on the bizarre but not so professionally trained as Dr. Puckett, recorded a huge number of Black disclaimers of magic.

The Rawick reprint of the slave narratives includes statements like "Thank God I'se had 'nough sense not to believe in haunts and sich things. I has 'possum hunt at night by myself in graveyards and I ain't seen one yet." Another ex-slave testified, "Never didn' believe in no conjurin. Don' care what they say bout it, . . . dey make a mistake to say somebody do somethin to dem. Ain' nobody but de Lord do nothin, I say."[16]

Thus the ascendancy of the superstitious over the traditionally positive African view was never complete, even among the most oppressed and frustrated Blackamericans, rural or urban. Most Blacks, in or out of slavery, resisted "conjure" or magic both because it so seldom seemed to be effective, and because it was contrary to the belief system and ethical rules of the higher tradition. There was and still is, of course, a tension between the low and the high religious traditions in the psyche of most Blacks, but the higher prevails. There are superstitious habits buried in my own unconscious that resist all high insight. I live *with* these habits but not *by* them. The experience of the descendants of North Europeans is no different. They feel strange when a black cat crosses their path, but such feelings do not order their lives. The preponderance of superstition in the literature by Whites about Blacks is a product of the writers' selectivity.

We have, then, two levels of Black belief. The lower is documented continuously from the preslavery African tradition to the present. The higher is well documented only in African oral tradition and in modern Black Christianity, starting with the abundant records of the nineteenth century. The hard data show similar content throughout the low-religion continuum, as well as similar content on the two ends of the high-religion tradition. It is ludicrous to suppose that the hole in the higher data continuum is anything more than the failure of biased, slave-owning writers to be sensitive to the high religion and deep faith of those they held as slaves. They *screened* for the bizarre in Black belief at every stage of their writing, and yet they "leaked" evidence of very high Black religion. They asked Blacks to pray for them, and they reported heroism and faith of the highest kind, often unaware of what it was. Puckett reported occasional examples of high religious views among Blacks, but he assumed it to be the shallow veneer of a lately acquired Christian faith among his informants. What he could not see was this continuously high religious view that had prevailed all along and that had filled the voids and sustained bruised and weary slaves long before they could express their beliefs in the language of the

King James Version of the Bible.

Perhaps the most complete and impressive evidence of the higher ideological continuum is the slaves' unrelenting resistance to slavery. No spiritual admonishes the acceptance of slavery, no matter how exclusively "otherworldly" it may have been mistakenly heard to be. Even under the constant supervision of Whites, and with the full awareness that there were Black informers, no Black preacher or exhorter dared preach an apparent acceptance of slavery unless he slipped in a few code reservations and encouragements to resistance. The ideological base for the thoroughly religious conviction that the African High God was opposed to American-style slavery was wholly independent of the high religion of Whites. Blacks later sought and easily found biblical proof texts for their conviction about slavery. The most obvious text was the Exodus story of the divine deliverance of the Jews from slavery in Egypt. "Let my people go," said a Negro spiritual. But the humane gospel of dignity and freedom crossed over from Africa with the slaves, and it never died.

This independence is evidenced by the frequent occurrence in slave narratives of strong preference for Black preachers rather than White. The Whites who were able to preach with any success at all noted that the response seemed to be to tonality, gesture, and emotion, as opposed to what they considered acceptable content. In their Euro-American ignorance they were unaware of the cultural signals by which they had inadvertently affirmed African identity. The sounds and signs that constituted a Black communications code, easily understood by members of the largely independent slave culture, were mistaken by Whites for gullibility and ignorance whereas in fact slaves were culturally almost self-sufficient and very intelligent. That they were perfectly capable of reading White faces and voices, and of sorting out biblical ideas, was proven more than once when they responded with utter indifference or even a foot vote (walking out) after an obnoxious pro-slavery "sermon."

To use this relatively solid data to suggest a continuum between the known in African tradition and the known in the folk

beliefs of nineteenth century Blackamericans (and those following) is not to suggest a total and isolated continuity, void of the
dynamics of cultural interplay. It is essential only to insist that
the meaning and impact of the belief base from Africa did not
die. These African roots play a significant part in the contrast
between Black and White Christian faith and life even today. On
the other hand it is also clear that some meanings died out completely. For instance, slave narratives frequently mention the pot
used to keep "ol' massa" from hearing unauthorized prayer and
praise meetings. Yet it is obvious that this ubiquitous practice
cannot be explained simply as a sound-deadening technique.
The only plausible explanation of the use of the pot is the fact
that it is still widely used in the traditional religions of Africa,
even though it has completely different meaning there. Having
myself often taken part in rites in Africa which employed the
pots, I can only assume that the explanation advanced by Rawick's research is correct: "Clearly, the iron pot of kettle is a
symbolic element, the original associations of which have been
lost."[17] There is quite a difference, however, between saying that
some meanings were lost and saying that all or most meanings
were lost.

The fact that the pot's significance was so different in this
country illustrates how impossible it would be to maintain any
hypothesis of total continuity. But the concession to the inevitable evolutions of living religions in no way destroys the validity
of the survival of many elements in adapted forms. The startling
similarities between African traditional funeral rites and Blackamerican practices are illustrative of meanings adapted but
largely retained. The extremes of grief expression and of later
celebration were misunderstood by the learned. The funeral rite
was and is helpful in grief, and it has been adapted and kept,
despite that fact that Black religion is nowhere more different
from White than in the rituals of the funeral. This is not total
continuity, but it is close enough for clear recognition. Indeed,
the claim to the survival of a brittle tradition would be hard to
sustain. The open and adaptive stance of the African mind, espe-

cially, supports the point. Rawick states it well concerning American Blacks when he says, that "if the ability of people to survive requires creative change adequate to the task at hand, then there is no more creative and innovative people in the New World than Black Americans."[18]

One other kind of data, the psychological, is also available. Wilmore alludes to it when he says that slavery only served to drive the influences of the African religious past underground. However, the force of terror and brutality did not decay the African residuum. Instead, it was "enhanced and strengthened in the subterranean vaults of the unconscious from which it arose—time and time again—during moments of greatest adversity and oppression—to subvert the attempt to make the slave an emasculated, second-class version of the white man."[19]

What Wilmore says about the so-called "unconscious" as the repository of the Black man's African religious heritage is highly significant. More and more scholars are coming to awareness that religion is not exclusively cerebral—that indeed much of every religion's most normative influence and insight emanates from the collective "unconscious" of its adherents. Harvey Cox, the Harvard theologian, is a good case in point. He, too, sees the Black man's religion, along with the White Appalachian's, as illustrative of the power and beauty and relevance of "unconscious" folk religion.[20]

However, I resist the term "unconscious," because it implies an aspect of personhood which is "unaware." Quite clearly this implication is not valid. While it contrasts with the *rational* conscious, this "unconscious" aspect of human personality is not *ir*-rational either. It simply has its own modes of intuitive perception and its own structures for ordering what is perceived. It has ideas, predispositions, experiences and a frame of reference with which to view the world. All these are stored in what might better be labeled the "transconscious." One might better state it that each person and each cultural group have a personal and a group psyche which reflect the experience and wisdom of the group through the ages. One need not affirm C. G. Jung's controversial archetypes (so closely associated with the "collective unconscious") to see that taboos and value judgments and other habitual responses to reality are communicated to succeeding generations, often nonverbally and without conscious intent. Every healthy Black has had many experiences which support Wilmore's assertion that much of the Black past is repressed to "unconscious" levels, only to surge forth in a crisis. This is what we mean when we say, "And just about that time my Black blood rose up." Some wisdom is captured and preserved in words, but much human behavior is governed by psychological and social patterns which are never consciously "learned."

One very concrete illustration of the collective transconscious is language. In it are imbedded whole frames of reference and a host of built in judgments. Sea Island Blacks who have only one personal pronoun for both sexes show, today, that in their ancestral tongue there was neither male nor female designation. Their root cultural world view would delight the most ardent women's libber. Again, African views of the unity of the sacred and secular often survive among the masses of Blackamericans. White Western ideologies descending from the classical Greek threaten and erode this unity by the very fact that the issue has to be stated in a non-African language of a race that takes the division for granted. But pervasive White dualism has not yet destroyed the wholeness of the Black "transconscious." What some think of as "Black rhythm" is really the fact that Blacks are completely at home in their bodies. Here, in body movements, a whole language and world view are resisted unaware.

As a matter of fact, much of the Black religious tradition continues unverbalized, a kind of alien outside the English language camp. For example the whole Black preaching tradition is just beginning to be analytically explored. Yet generation after generation of Black preachers have literally caught the subtleties of Black imagery, motif, and timing. The life story of most effective Black preachers will show that they learned it not at school but from a father or other close and contagious bearer of the preaching tradition. Baptist preachers' kids (BPK's) like Malcolm X,

Ron Karenga, and Huey Newton have not followed their fathers into the ministry, but they have had an impressive track record in the use of their unconsciously acquired wisdom about the charismatic communication of critical concerns. The Black "rap" or verbal tradition is rich, but there is much "between the lines" and "off the page," *non*verbally communicated.

Black psychological research (into the structure and inventory of the Black collective unconscious and its interpersonal and intergenerational processes) will no doubt add much to our self-understanding, both for survival and for liberation. But what we can see already explains and confirms a great deal about the unconscious religious reservoirs and about the tenacity of Black culture and world view. And the unconscious will come up again and again in the consideration of tenacity.

Tenacity of Culture

To kill a culture you have to kill the bearers of that culture. That is to say, the life stance and world view of a people are deeply ingrained and not readily changed. To have life is to depend on these defenses and, as we have already said, pressure to destroy them often succeeds only in driving them underground. Much of a people's culture is therefore outside rational consciousness. It is transmitted from "unconscious" to "unconscious," as well as from rational conscious to rational conscious. To stamp out a culture and its world view would require total genocide, or total and permanent separation of all bearers and receivers. This would have to include separation of all babies from their culture-bearing mothers at birth, regardless of the identity of the father. This is a virtual impossibility although groups such as the Nazis have tried. There is more and more evidence that slave mothers, and sometimes fathers too, participated in the raising of their children. The passing on of a culture and world view were inevitable, and the fact that slaves were in constant contact with new arrivals bearing African culture, only added to the life expectancy of the Black way of seeing things.

That anybody should ever hypothesize otherwise seems to me more than passing strange. To do so flies in the face of over-whelming general evidence to the contrary. For instance, Christianity had long since "converted" Europe when New England Puritan Christians were still drowning or hanging witches. That pre-Christian piece of world view is dying hard, and it is only one European superstition which is still very much alive in our culture. People somehow don't apply the word "heathen" to superstition until it is found in a culture other than their own. The fact is, then, that Africans inevitably believed some of the same kinds of superstitions; but they also kept quite a bit of that which was already on par with the Christian revelation. To start at the most obvious level, lowest African belief was at least as compatible with Christianity as the well-known examples in America of superstitious English (and other) cultural tenacity—the idea that black cats bring bad luck if they happen to cross one's path,[21] or the idea that the world is overrun with evil witches and other spirits.[22] Conviction of being a witch was worthy of death by lynching if detected by English or American citizens of the seventeenth or eighteenth century. The main point, however, is simply that the gospel of Christ himself has not been able to kill off any culture's magical beliefs in one quick stroke, or even in centuries of hard preaching and teaching. This is significant evidence.

The existence of higher African religion on a theological par with Christianity adds to the inevitable tenacity of African belief since America's "Christian" cultural context overlaps and supports the African. Joseph R. Washington, Jr., holds strongly to the discontinuity of African content, but he is not the least in doubt about this compatibility.[23] Black historian Carter G. Woodson quoted an early eighteenth-century missionary in South Carolina as saying that "while so many professed Christians among Whites were lukewarm, it pleased God to raise himself devout servants among the heathen [!!], whose faithfulness was commended among the masters themselves."[24] Woodson rightly held that African slaves were especially well oriented to high religion and, thus, easily able to continue expressing their religious bent within a "Christian" society. The overwhelming general evidence does not restrict itself to the model of pre-Christian European folk culture's tenacity. There is evidence internal to Black faith.

Related to this evidence in Blackamerican folk religion is the cultural tenacity inside modern African Christianity. Many African religious groups combine the same African and Euro-American elements as does the folk faith of American Blacks. Thus these contemporary indigenous adaptations can serve as significant models of the religious acculturation process. African faiths are especially helpful as tracers of the survival tendencies of higher traditional religion under fire. E. Frankin Frazier claims "that with the breaking up or destruction of the clan and kinship organization [of the Fon people of Dahomey], the religious myths and cults lost their significance."[25] My own experience with African religious groups would lead me to believe that this dislocation, rather than creating the vacuum assumed by Frazier, triggered an adaptive response. In other words, the breaking up of traditional kinship and folk faith structures did not terminate the African villager's religious drive and deeply spiritual world view. Their belief simply surfaced in West Africa's large cities in the form of a vast variety of strongly African cults. Many if not most of them are also markedly Christian. All of them could be said to create in the urban setting a working substitute for the social stability of the traditionally religious tribal or extended family life. Many of these cults also stand consciously over against the unbelievably cold and Europeanized Christianity of most of the missionary churches. The religious persistence evidenced by these cults, together with their admirable creativity and adaptive skills, can hardly be assumed to have been possessed only by the Africans who were not sent over as slaves.

John S. Mbiti, Kenyan author of three volumes on African religion, supports this reading of the cults. He says that these "independent church movements" are attempts to establish a *substitute* for the disintegrating traditional society. The rather small groups of Black storefronts, provide a haven where uprooted men and women find some comfort, a sense of belonging together, a feeling of oneness, and acceptance of themselves and their culture.[26]

On the basis of what I have seen on both sides of the Atlantic, this suggests that when Fon kinship groups, myths, and cults lost their literal significance as a result of the dislocations of European influence, they followed the standard African pattern. The vast majority of those who did not become culturally Western, adapted and invented another faith and family group out of the materials at hand rather than sink into meaninglessness and despair. When America's southern rural Blacks had to face the same dislocation and supposed disintegration of myths in the move to the northern industrial cities, the same response was evident. It is therefore unthinkable that the same drive and adaptability were not employed in the solution of the problems posed by forced migration to overseas slave plantations.

Once one sees this indomitable drive, and this cultural demand for a religious and familial frame of reference, it is not hard to see how slaves seized and adapted American Christian faith forms even before they were welcomed to them, and before they were legally recognized as having souls. The fact that Whites did take religious initiative is obvious. Lawrence N. Jones has said that "the fifty thousand Blacks . . . who had become Christian in 1800, did so in spite of, rather than because of the evangelists."[27] The way in which they approached it has been stated in the DuBois quotation above,[28] and in my own statement about West African openness to new religious ideas. Another and more detailed description of the same kind of process is spelled out skillfully in Mbiti's description of the way in which Africans respond today to the confrontation between culture-religions. He names two categories of religion growing out of the process:

[1] *Contact Religion* is the type in which a person feels no contradiction in holding a mixture of belief and practice from two or more religious

traditions in Africa. As we have seen, Christianity, Islam, and traditional religions overlap in a number of points, and this makes it fairly easy for a person to be a convinced Christian or Muslim and yet incorporate in his life elements from the traditional religions. He may have a Christian or Muslim name, may wear a crucifix or a Muslim cap, but beyond these badges he would know little else about the depths of Christianity or Islam even if he may be devoted to either. His unconscious life is deeply traditional, but his waking life is oriented towards one of the world religions. He has established a link and a contact with two or more systems; and it is in this context of that "contact religion" that he identifies himself and his interests.

[2] *Instant Religion* is that which shows itself mainly in moments of crisis . . . and comes to the surface also at key moments of life like birth, wedding, death. . . . Such moments call for "instant prayer" and "instant God." . . . Both educated and village dwellers in Africa subscribe to this type of religion.[29]

Our Blackamerican foreparents no doubt had similar responses to the two religions in their lives, when most Blacks, with the exception of those steeped in Western culture, still have vestigal remains of the two. How could it be otherwise when, as Washington suggests, Blacks were ignored and left to "work out their own religious response to their peculiar experience in America."[30] In the century and a half of which there is so little religious record, Blacks, as DuBois suggested, moved more and more to the externals of their "contact religion," which was Christianity. But they have not yet lost their "instant religion," which greatly affects how they interpret and practice their Christianity.

A church in an area where I once served exemplified the lower aspect of this "instant religion" in the ouster of a pastor, just prior to my arrival on the area staff. As nearly as I could find out, he had been effective in the Black idiom—a good preacher. Whatever weaknesses he may have had otherwise, he had been popular with the majority. So, although there were thoughtful critics or opponents of the pastor, they failed to convince the rank and file that he was unfit. Finally, the restrained but persistent criticism aroused the pastor's deepest fears. Thereupon he re-

verted to his Louisiana instant religion and employed all the
remedies he had known, to protect himself and his position.

When a church member caught him planting charms at the
four corners of the church and another detected that he had
"dusted" the communion table after it was set, many refused to
receive "sacrament." Others refused so much as to enter the
building. It was an easy matter, then, to get a virtually unani-
mous vote for his removal, on grounds of his departure from
sound doctrine. But I was never able to escape the impression
that unorthodoxy was really only an excuse. Deep fear of the
pastor's possible powers in the occult were the actual basis for
his ouster. His acts had called forth all the unconscious world
view that the most sophisticated thought they had outgrown or
forgotten. Such is the cultural two-headedness and tenacity of
Black religion.

There is, however, one very significant difference between the
cultural processes on the two sides of the ocean. In the United
States language needs, in the absence of a West African common
tongue, had a significant effect on the appearance of belief. The
only language to which the slaves could turn was English in most
of the colonies, so they had no choice but to "paste" English/Ch-
ristian labels on their concepts and feelings of whatever cultural
origin. Thus there was an appearance of a complete shift from
the African faith-base. It was very misleading, especially when
compared to the processes in Africa, where an alien *missionary*
learned the *native* tongue. Ironically, the Blacks in the United
States had more integrity and content retention, even though
they were in a strange land, because they (and not missionaries)
controlled the translation into English.

An illustration of how misleading cultural subtleties like this
can be is Frazier's contention that shouting and spirit possession
were culturally stripped from Blacks and then learned again
under White auspices. Frazier argued that we may dismiss such
speculations as the one that slave response to Methodist and
Baptist missionary work was due to their African background.
"We are on sounder ground when we note . . . that [they] appealed

to the poor and the ignorant and the outcast." "In the emotionalism of the camp meetings and revivals some social solidarity, even if temporary, was achieved."[31] For Frazier, the similarities of emotional intensity among unlearned and poor Whites and Blacks was adequate reason to assign responsibility for the whole phenomenon to the Whites who, on the surface, were in charge.

It is true, of course, that the roots of shouting White Methodism have been clearly established to be in Ireland and Wales,[32] where shouting appeared prior to American White contact with the spirit-possessed Blacks from Africa. But that is not enough to justify Frazier's assumption that Blacks *re*learned spirit possession after a total disjuncture. I know they didn't because I can still see the subtle differences in the motor habits of possessed Whites and Blacks.

But far more important is the well-documented fact that from the beginning, no matter how well supervised, the slaves never gave up their rites of spirit possession, such as ring shouting. As will be seen in detail later, the slow-moving circle, with the beat supplied by hands and feet (now that the African drum was outlawed), never stopped from the early start of the "pagan" rites slaves held and masters tried to suppress. Although shouting is often associated largely with women, Black soldiers in the Civil War had ring shouts and were ecstatically possessed in camp every night they weren't engaged in battle or at the ready. These Sea Island soldiers had never seen a frontier revival, and very few Whites save their restrained and aristocratic masters and their families. Their only possible source was their African background. There is also abundant evidence of the African roots out of which ring shouts and possession came. The literature on African possession is ample. Much of the description of Fanti possession given by Christensen will sound very familiar to any Black Baptist or Methodist, and certainly any Pentecostal.[33]

One of the most interesting stories in the whole literature on the Black church in America is Bishop Smith's record of Daniel

Payne's attempt to squelch a ring shout in 1878. The venerable and learned Dr. Payne was visiting a church on the Baltimore Circuit of the African Methodist Episcopal church when he saw what he called a "heathenish" thing. After the sermon the folk took off their coats and formed a ring. Then they "stamped" their feet, clapped their hands and sang. The bishop ordered the pastor to stop this disgraceful dancing and have them sit and sing. In deference to Bishop Payne they surrendered the circle, but they refused to sit and sullenly walked away. It took fifteen minutes and more than one request to accomplish this much. That afternoon Bishop Payne engaged the ringleader in conversation, reminding him that only the Spirit of God and the word of God can convert sinners. The leader agreed, but insisted that for the Spirit to do this very thing there simply had to be not one ring but many.

No matter how many rings may have been formed in the British Isles, there is no question whatever but that these AME shouting rings were transplants from Africa. Payne clearly hinted his knowledge of their source, referring to them as "voodoo dance"; and he complained that some of the most powerful and popular preachers specialized in this "fanaticism." The poor words to some of their songs were doubtless reason enough for the bishop's concern, but it is at least odd that he never seemed aware that the word African in the denomination's title might be taken seriously.[34]

In January, 1974 I had the privilege of seeing a similar scene, in a different place and denomination. The Annual Conference of the African Methodist Episcopal Zion Church in Kingston, Jamaica, West Indies, was presided over by the venerable Bishop Herbert Bell Shaw, of New York. The AME Zion churches of Jamaica are new to the conference, and they have brought with them a stronger African influence than is common in the United States. They had a ring shout right in the annual meeting, with the bishop consenting, even presiding in this case. I had to admire the Black cultural integrity of Bishop Shaw, but I was most moved by the privilege of seeing my religious heritage in living color. It was preserved by islanders in a majority Black population, deeply Christian members of a truly *African* Methodist Church. Their theological statements were no doubt far superior to those that would have been made by Bishop Payne's members a century ago. But they had seen no reason why this should stop a tradition from Africa which had been found to be spiritually effective.

The rubrics "tenacity of culture" and "instant religion" invite one further comment and qualification. Whereas African traditional religions were the instant religion of the slaves, the Black religious tradition, a fusion of African and biblical Christian elements, has become the instant religion of the Blackamerican three hundred years later. As the modern Black faces a secularized White majority culture, often being drawn into its deadly cold intellectual labyrinth, he may bow the knee to such new contact religions as humanism, agnosticism, nihilism, or dialectical materialism. Or, in another pattern, he may become a self-conscious, antiecclesiastical street-culture Black militant. Another route is that of the escapist, with or without drink or drug dependence. But, like his Black forebears, in a crisis he will still unconsciously utter, "Have mercy!" and fall back onto his culture's prevailing world view or instant religion.

I have carefully avoided using the words reversion or regression here because instant religion is not necessarily regressive to lower belief levels and superstition. An illustration of this slipping "up" to a higher level occurred, and perhaps still does, in a Brooklyn hospital maternity ward. At the time the nurse told me of it, I was not aware of its full significance, but I never forgot it. She had been comparing the reactions of mothers of the various ethnocultural groups, while they were going through labor pains. She had found that there were fairly predictable responses and expressions in the crisis, according to the group from which these common folk came. The nurse was shocked to find one group of mothers who habitually cursed their husbands for causing the pregnancy and, therefore, the pain. They seemed to have no sense of the sacredness of the moment. On the other hand, the nurse, a Black herself, was most astonished by the reaction of Black mothers. Her report was that no matter how much of a "tramp" the Black mother might be—a prostitute, shoplifter, addict, or all three—or if she had never been to church or had any religious training, when the pains were worst she would still cry out, "Have mercy, Lord!" Out of her transconscious, in the height of crisis, came the Black religion that is so high and yet so tenacious. I have recently checked this reading of instant or "unconscious" folk Christianity among Blacks from coast to coast. The only change is that it applies to all pain and not just labor. And it applies to Black men as well as women.

Contemporary Black instant religion includes undeniable White influence, such as words to blackenized or gospelized hymns, but the Black spiritual world view is at the bottom of it all. And the crosscultural influence works in both directions. It is probable that Borneman is nearest the truth when he says that "the Methodist revival movement began to address itself directly to the slaves, but ended up not by converting the Africans to Christian ritual, but by converting itself to an African ritual."[35]

Borneman's field of interest is jazz music, which Imamu Amiri Baraka, formerly LeRoi Jones, quite rightly holds to be an accurate index to the acculturative process. The odd fact is that so many accept the tenacity of culture when applied to a concrete musical sound, but deny it in relation to high religious ideas. It is common knowledge that Africans came to America with a different view of the role of music and different instruments and vocal traditions—even different scales. But there seems to be no problem with calling Black jazz a synthesis of two cultures, still very heavily influenced by its African roots. There should be no more of a problem in affirming this process to be true of Blackamerican religion.

As Baraka points out, there are various types or strains of Black music; and the same is true of Black religion. No cultural or religious tradition so adaptive and so given to improvisation could or should be expected to be monolithic in its music or its religion. One of the strains of the Black religious tradition, the most common in fact, shows a higher intensity of African influence in the higher frequency of shouting/possession as a religious expression and this is only one aspect of the survival of higher religion.

Significance of the Folklore Studies

One of the richest sources of insight into the African-American continuum is found in the materials gathered by folklorists and cultural anthropologists. By definitions current at the time of the major works, folklore consists of the "traditional customs, beliefs, tales, or sayings, especially those of a superstitious or legendary nature, preserved unreflectively among a people."[36] This definition implies highly selective and disparaging implications about the type of customs sought out by the folklore discipline but the fact remains that the momumental task of gathering field data at a time when direct sources still survived, was accomplished primarily by folklorists. Even the slave narratives of the WPA (Rawick) fall into this category.

Perhaps the best known and most comprehensive of the studies is Newbell Niles Puckett's *The Magic and Folk Beliefs of the Southern Negro.* Puckett has established beyond any possible doubt, both by intent and by apparently unconscious implication, that there was a large body of remedies, signs, stories, and superstitions from West Africa very much alive among the last slaves and their children. Puckett's detailed coverage includes some sound theories of interpretation, such as the idea that "only African beliefs of a universal nature would be likely to survive unless, perchance, many slaves from the same African locality were grouped together on a single plantation."[37] The latter was generally not true for slaves from the same language areas were carefully separated. (Bastide takes this fact into account in tracing the dominance of one West African culture over others in the New World, on the basis of a more localized universality.)[38] Puckett was also aware of a large body of corresponding folk belief which was present both in West Africa and in Europe, apparently independent of each other, and it was on this that he based his statement. In addition he found English and other European superstitions which, he said, found ready reception among the slaves, being of the same general type which they had brought with them.

Puckett concedes that "conjure" was an African survival and that it was not the major religion of Blacks.[39] He seems unaware, however, that the "subordinate" and very questionable position of conjure in the Black folk religion was exactly the same as its position in African traditional religion. In fact, ATR had and has as we have seen, far more stringent rules against evil magic. When the spiritual says that "Satan is a conjurer," the view reflects African no less than American Christian insight.

Puckett raises the issue of chance and uncertainty as contributing to the increase of superstition.[40] But he is wrong to suggest that the oppression of Blacks in the South was less threatening than the stable if technically underdeveloped existence of an African extended family. Thus he is led to the subsequent error of assuming that superstition had a lower status in Blackamerican belief than in African traditional religion. Often the very opposite was true. The influence of African "traditions of the past" is rightly acknowledged to be part of the Black interpretation of Christianity, but the level of that influence is grossly misjudged as being all low and superstitious.

Puckett is correct when he points out that the house servant was more influenced by *White* superstition than the field worker. He has indicated also, with a candor uncommon for a Mississippian in 1925, that superstition was *encouraged* by slave masters because of its usefulness in discipline.[41] However, he states that he has focused on folklore and superstition because almost everywhere else, the "African element has been entirely supplanted by the European."[42] In other words, any high religion or other achievement was assumed to be the result of White influence.

Puckett later says that these survivals consist almost entirely of matters relating to self-gratification and the supernatural, spheres in which Black life was less subject to White supervision and domination. Then he admits that to Whites, *any* African religious survival is automatically considered superstition, "the same belief being religion to one folk and superstition to another."[43] Thus he calls attention to the biases of lesser White minds, and then quietly indulges in others of his own. All the while he is guilty of the subtle sin of using Black culture as a way of studying culture processes for his own ends. He never looks at Black culture for its own sake.

Puckett adds error and confusion to bias when he asks why it was "necessary for the slave to *add* superstition to his early religion."[44] In answer to this question he explains that West African religions were an everyday affair, ministering to almost every exigency in practical life, whereas Christianity has a tendency to "deal with the hereafter rather than the here-and-now." The error persists when he speaks of *"supplementing* Christianity with superstition" later, indicating that the form of Christianity to which he refers was more of the Middle Ages. The reverse of this process, of course, was true. It was the Christianity that was added. Ironically, this section of his book was introduced with a statement that when "the African first landed on our shores he had only what we American would call pure superstition. Later there was a blending of superstition and Christianity, as he gradually assimilated the white man's creed and credulences."[45]

However, this confusion and bias is nowhere near as bad as the racial stereotype he uses in speaking of Blacks.

Laziness is found both in Africa and in America; in Africa being enhanced by the enervating tropical climate. . . . Sexual indulgence of the Negro, so open in Africa and in many parts of the rural South, may conceivably be a racial characteristic developed by natural selection in West Africa as a result of the frightful mortality. . . . Despotism in West Africa seems to win loyalty, pride, and popularity, possibly because a strong-minded master has spirit enough . . . to protect his followers from outside annoyance.[46]

Puckett explains or excuses each stereotypical sin ascribed to Blacks so as to seem psychologically to justify it. The explanations only compound the insult by means of "documentation."

It is a tragedy that this massive research was colored by such patent errors. West African proverbs abound with exhortations against laziness. The lazy man is perhaps the man most abhorred by the traditional society. Again, nobody at all familiar with the mores of West Africa would describe them as sexually indulgent. West African ideas about when to marry are different, but their concepts of responsibility and their rigid means of enforcement make Americans of any recent generation look like wicked libertines. And how could anybody familiar with the Ashanti political tradition believe that they like despots? They have the most sophisticated ways I know of for speaking about and dealing with power. One proverb says it is like an egg: if you grasp it too tightly you will break it, and if you hold it too loosely, you will drop it and break it. The Akan had a well-known way of offering power-hungry rulers a proposition they couldn't refuse: either they commit suicide or there will be an unexplained and uninvestigated homicide. Few if any civilizations have had more of a sense of responsibility in work and sex, or such guarantees against despotism. Puckett was apparently deceived by the African protocols of obeisance before their chiefs.

The internal ideals and purposes of the culture seem largely to be ignored by Puckett and other scholars. Higher forms such as wise proverbs are overlooked, and no part of the corpus of tradition is seen as a reservoir of folk theology. Indeed, whether the editors of books of proverbs were White or Black, the ones I own were all written as texts for language, not ethics and certainly not high belief. This is still another way of saying that *Blacks in Africa and America are seldom taken seriously.*

This evaluation of folklore as a resource is based, therefore, on more than a Black man's romantic desire to upgrade the image of Black religion and/or establish a continuum of that religion from Africa to America. Blacks, like all other healthy human beings, live by what they trust rather than by what they fear. To be sure, they have had enough peripheral superstitions to tickle the ear of the folklorist, and they were not notably articulate in expressing their faith to Whites seeking knowledge of high beliefs. But many a saintly slave and Black believer had a genius for faith at its very highest levels, known and expressed only in "folk" as opposed to "theological" terms. It is high time this faith was taken seriously and allowed to teach mankind, rather than simply providing grist for the mill of lesser intellectual objectives. Such prostitution of Black culture and belief has consistently meant that the researchers ask the wrong questions, and that guarantees that they will get the wrong answers from a Black perspective.

Wrong questions generate wrong emphases as well. Puckett, along with the collectors of hundreds of slave narratives I have read, was seeking odd folk "remedies," not folk *medicine*. Thus, of sugar and alum as remedies for postnatal hemorrhage, Puckett could say that Black midwives were "under the *impression* [italics mine] that it hastens the curative process."[47] Any man with an I.Q. of seventy-five or better, who shaves with a blade, should know that styptic pencils made of that same alum contract blood vessels and stop bleeding. So does the tannic acid in the bark tea prescribed by Black midwives, a remedy taken lightly by Puckett. And I have personally seen medical doctors prescribe sugar packing to heal the bed sores of elderly patients. It was impossible for the folklorist to see the technical excellence of this African remedy because, to him, folk healing is all "folk" and not real medicine.

That there should be such concrete scientific validation of African cures should come as no surprise. All folk medicine has been effective enough to keep its folk practitioners and their people alive and well to greet the arrival of the "scientific" age. The African race, if different, has only been on the earth longer and has had more time to employ its creativity and pragmatism in the development of herbal and other cures. These methods were complicated enough to require three years of training for priests who also served as doctors and who are erroneously referred to as "witch doctors." Who knows how much of the medical genius of highly advanced Timbuktu had gravitated southward, to West Africa's coastal kingdoms? It is already well established that this Arab-African medical knowledge was also carried to the north to provide a base for later European medicine.

At Mampong, near the city of Accra, Ghana, lives a great and famous physician and surgeon, Dr. Oku Ampofo. He has a hospital and dispensary (pharmacy) according to the best European medical traditions. But he also is doing serious research to find out why some of the traditional cures of his people are so effective. Patients are said to have the option to select free traditional medicine whenever possible. The surgeon is a magnificent humanitarian, drawing both from his European training and his own fathers' wisdom (after the manner of Chinese surgeons using acupuncture), and adding quiet Black self-esteem to the best of the two traditions. He is not only a better physician and surgeon for it, but he lives a more abundant life, which includes his talent as one of the finest sculptors in all of Africa.

While folklorists have grossly misjudged effective Black religion-medicine as "magic," their misperception of the healing and high religious content of spirit possession has been far worse. Puckett describes Black-culture Holy Spirit possessions in rural Mississippi as frenzy, sensuous emotion, superstitious trances, and hypnotic religious power. His one sound contribution is his specific relating of this phenomenon to possession traditions in Nigeria and Ghana.[48] Although this assumption of the African-American connection is far from unique to Puckett, the idea is particularly important here, since I know of no adequate study of Blackamerican Holy Spirit possession. Because of the tie, one can utilize the excellent studies of the Haitian voodoo stage in the linkage between the African and the Blackamerican possession traditions.

For instance, Puckett would agree with anthropologists Sheila S. Walker and Maya Deren that possession is the supreme act of worship in African and Blackamerican tradition. Yet he would deny entirely their reading of the possession experience as related to reality in any way save escape. Deren and Walker join in a firm finding that possession *helps* people in their everyday concerns. However, Walker and Deren themselves have interesting differences on how this help and healing are accomplished.

Walker employs psychoanalytic terminology to describe it. "Instead of the seemingly flat and incomplete technique of trying to express one's unconscious self only verbally while lying on an analyst's couch isolated from society, the possessed individual expresses himself with his whole body through drama and dance in a situation involving the people with whom he normally interacts." She suggests that the very personality of the loa or deity by whom one is possessed is chosen to express the yearnings and feelings of the devotee.[49] The ritualized catharsis is safely nonspecific and done in a highly supportive context of one's peers. I hardly need add that the same is true of possession or shouting in the Blackamerican churches.

Deren, who is White but has participated in Haitian voodoo and has been authentically possessed, insists that the Western analytic approach does not apply. In the first place, "primitive" people have very few neuroses—"a relatively meager unconscious." For Deren, they are simply and literally ridden or possessed by the loa. The personality of the loa replaces and transcends their own. Just to be indwelt by these spiritual embodiments of cosmic good is the major blessing. It "comprehends all minor needs." Quite naturally the loa come bearing advice, prescriptions and discipline, but this is secondary. If health, for instance, comes, it is not the *result* of a ritual action, it is the *reward.*[50]

Walker and Deren do agree, then, that the possession experience is supportive of oppressed humanity, affirming personhood and healing persons. They also agree generally that the ego or a subsystem of it is surrendered in the process. Deren would insist in addition, from her deep involvement in the experience, that possession is of the highest order of religion, and that it provides guidance for life from transcendent sources. Being deeply involved in the possession tradition of Blackamerican Christianity, I would heartily agree, saying the same and more of the possession of the Holy Spirit.

Misjudgment persists in the pervasive assumption that even such a "marginal" phenomenon as conjure is exclusively devoted to individual problems and/or unworthy ends. In reality, conjure was often used as a resource in social goals far more worthy than those of the slavemaster's "high" religion.

When Denmark Vesey was putting together a slave revolt in Charleston, South Carolina, in 1822, his mostly African Methodist Episcopal church conspiracy included Gullah Jack, an expert in African folk methods of dealing with the psychic needs of people in a crisis. He rendered Christians who were on risky assignments invulnerable by putting a crab claw in their mouths. The fact that the revolt failed was not due to mistaken dependence on this conjure. The plot was simply exposed in advance and thwarted by massive force.

As a boy Frederick Douglass had a more successful experience with a conjure for the purposes of resistance. He had been mercilessly driven beyond his endurance, and cruelly beaten by a slave breaker named Covey, to whom he had been contracted. Douglass had struggled back to the home of his owner, who was kinder on the surface, only to be returned summarily to the impossible situation at Covey's. Young Frederick escaped a second time, and found temporary refuge with Sandy, another slave. Under the circumstances it was difficult not to accept Sandy's offer of an African root charm, which, Sandy said, would guarantee him against any further beatings, provided he carried it on his right side. Douglass actually followed these instructions and was never beaten again. Of course, being even then a very literate fellow, Douglass had other ways of explaining the success of the charm. These would have included his own physical resistance and Covey's embarrassment at not being able to subdue him. But one can easily understand Sandy's strong conviction that the root had been the critical factor in Fred's deliverance.[51] The young and intellectual orator later confessed his inability to prove otherwise, and the vast majority of slaves would have agreed easily with Sandy. They expected this kind of result, and they were not disappointed in enough instances for them to lose an African religious tradition which held that there were forces in the universe available for the moral causes of men.

When positive readings such as this appear they are generally accidental. Thus, Puckett reported that "the fetish-man or medium is not a witch. Consulting and enlisting spirits in self-defense or for blessings is considered a duty, not a crime. But the misuse of a spiritual influence for bringing harm, especially sickness and death, on one's fellow-creatures is the most heinous crime."[52]

That this positive evidence is accidental is evident in this ironical sequel, to be found on the very same page, alleging that "we must remember that the African gods are not concerned with moral practices." One would search Puckett in vain for an application of folk belief to a moral cause such as Black liberation. He may have one good excuse, however. What sane Black man in the deep South would have told a White folk researcher about his high goals of freedom in the 1920s?

It takes a Black scholar to elicit accurate answers from Black folk sources and to interpret them as well. Gayraud S. Wilmore's reading of the morality of slave and African folk religion is far more accurate. "What both the slave churches of the South—'the invisible institution'—and the free churches of the North developed was a religion suffused with a sublimated outrage that was balanced with a patient cheerfulness and boundless confidence in the ultimate justice [morality] of God."[53]

Wilmore carefully suggests that scholars of disciplines other than his own field of ethics are better fitted to describe and research "the African religious background, which provided a rapidly disintegrating but persistently influential base upon which the religious institutions of the slave were based."[54] But he has some pointed comments, nevertheless, on the issue of morality in African and Afro-American folk belief. He reminds the reader that African religions know no rigid demarcation between natural and supernatural, or sacred and profane. The world of spirits, forces, or powers, so strange to the rational conscious mind of Western man, has great influence on man's welfare. One must commune with the spirits properly. Wilmore corrects the common view of the African voodoo religion of Haiti, clearly stating that it is not just a strategy for vengeance, "but as much a moral religion as the Christianity of the plantation owners and missionaries. The voodoo was a god of goodness, not of satanic evil. . . . the spirits do not engage in criminal acts, but behave in conformity with the normative mores and conventions of society."[55]

Wilmore well illustrates the independence and initiative, as well as self-confidence, which a Black scholar must have in order to see the positive in a forest of White bias. In addition to the racist basis for error there is also a considerable number of "honest" mistakes—the ones born of understandable White ignorance of the subtleties and nuances which would be easily known and understood by one inside the Black culture. One can miss a great deal because of the limitations of the "motifs" or typologies into which White folklorists classify all their data. The point is simply that until "scholarship" is restructured and even redefined, by Blacks and for Blacks, its findings will fly wide of the mark in both truth and usefulness. What data folklore and cognate fields provide will continue to require considerable reinterpretation, because the vast resources employed, even today, are often used to ask the wrong questions. What we have learned from folklore, therefore, greatly helps to confirm the African-American continuum in high religious content, but it also suggests a need for a major revolution in White "scholarship," present and future.

Conclusion

When a whole people have been cast in a dehumanized role, it should not be surprising that their profoundest concerns and folk expressions should have been heard inaccurately and never taken seriously. Indeed, it should come as no shock that Blacks themselves have taken so long to recognize the cultural and spiritual integrity of their foreparents. The massive bias has been, as we have seen, written into so many sources that few souls have had the courage and intellectual stamina of a DuBois or a Woodson. And even they have been tainted somewhat by the language of their time, a real problem even in the Bible. Words like heathen and pagan die hard. Nevertheless, there is a store of both direct and circumstantial evidence, that should lay to rest forever the unchallenged idea that Blacks were stripped religiously and culturally on any level, high or low. And the high religion continuum of Afro-Americans must be examined more thoroughly than has the magic and superstition of Blacks.

The overlooking of high religion may, however, be a blessing in disguise, in that White domination of the literature on early Black folk belief is limited to surface aspects. This leaves it up to Black scholars to do the pioneer work on the higher and more controlling folk beliefs. The very first works of any size and significance can then be based on understandings, feelings, and memory *interior* to the tradition of Black folk belief. As one who has lived in that tradition for over half a century and practiced ministry in its churches for thirty years, I must do my best to accomplish a start in this direction.

THREE

African Roots of American Black Belief

Despite all the obvious changes in modern Africa, traditional religious views linger on with great tenacity. This is cogently expressed by J. S. Mbiti: "In my description I have generally used the present tense, as if these ideas are still held and the practices being carried out." Answering the apparent challenge of the rapid changes taking place in Africa, he says that

it would be wrong to imagine that everything traditional has been changed or forgotten. . . . If anything, the changes are generally on the surface, affecting the material side of life, and only beginning to reach the deeper levels of thinking pattern, language content, mental images, emotions, beliefs and response in situations of need. Traditional concepts still form the essential background."[1]

The obviously early vintage of much contemporary culture and religion in West Africa would lead the sensitive observer to realize that Professor Mbiti has stated it well. The change rate is still slow, and the proportion of the contrasting Western-oriented community is still very small, especially in deep beliefs. What we learn of African folk religion is, then, in a kind of timeless dimension—a miraculously available "instant replay" of life from half a millennium ago. What takes place today in West Africa, at least for now, may be properly relied upon as representative of the beliefs of the African forebears of modern Blackamericans.

In addition to my personal research in Africa the sources for this survey of folk roots consist of written records of phenomena such as creation myths, the vast array of praise-names for God, proverbs, oral tradition, and social customs.[2] No African Aquinas has attempted to force all, or even part, of this oral tradition into a Western-style "summa theologica." The most useful approach, then, would seem to be to make a strategic selection of topics and deal with them by quotation from the traditional religions of West Africa, together with necessary commentary. The major topics tend to divide into types. Praise-names provide most of the direct doctrine about God, with proverbs implying much about the nature of reality and life. Proverbs seldom speak of God directly, their wisdom and ethics being largely situational, but revealing a value system of great yet subtle theological significance. Both praise-names and proverbs have a direct relationship to biblical Christianity and especially to American Black folk Christianity.

This relationship between African slave-zone and Blackamerican folk belief may be stated thus:

1. African peoples do not know how to exist without religion.[3] Blackamericans have started the Western trek to secularization, but it is plain that they are far from finished.

A highly organized society predicated on the existence of mystical, omniscient superior beings who are in complete control of the lives and fates of all humans might seem a trifle "primitive" if viewed through the eyes of a society whose existence is predicated on exactly opposite hypotheses . . . a culture which forwards the "ultimate happiness of mankind" as the sole purpose of the universe. . . . The cult of man must view the cult of the divine as absurd.[4]

West African folk and Blackamericans still bear the stamp of the cult of the divine.

2. African religions have a great compatibility with biblical (originally folk) Christianity, as opposed to any special theologi-

cal interpretation which may predominate in Western culture. African scholars of religion, Protestant and Catholic, concur in this. E. Bolaji Idowu, Yoruba (Western Nigeria) scholar of religion, recognizes "the radical quality of God's self-revelation in Jesus Christ; and yet it is because of this revelation we can discern what is truly of God in our pre-Christian heritage: this knowledge of God is not totally discontinuous with our people's previous traditional knowledge of Him."[5]

Stephan N. Ezeanya, Ibo (Eastern Nigeria) Catholic scholar, unhampered by Pope Pius XII's unfortunate use of the word "wild," quotes his strong statement of 1951 on traditional religion as cultural and religious base for Christianity: "Let not the gospel on being introduced into any new land destroy or extinquish whatever its people possess that is naturally good, just or beautiful. For the Church . . . does not act like one who recklessly cuts down and uproots a thriving forest. No, she grafts a good scion upon the wild stock that it may bear a crop of more delicious fruit."[6]

3. *The deepest concerns and the most profound beliefs of the Blackamerican folk religionist still largely parallel the emphases of traditional African high religion.* It would be hard to find anywhere near the same parallel to the typical concerns of the majority of White Christians.

4. The pull of African world view is still evident even in Blackamerican street culture, among those who have made a break with formal Black religion and the organized Black church.

As a result of this impressive kinship between African traditional religion and Christianity as perceived by Blacks, the following treatment of the African roots is often couched in the terms of the Bible—the English oral tradition of the transplanted African. There is no valid alternative. If this survey were stated in indigenous African languages, no American and few Africans outside the community of the language used would understand it. The European theological terms currently in vogue are both strange to the layperson and loaded with implications alien to Black belief on either side of the Atlantic. The one tongue closest to Blackamerican belief among the masses and to the folk wisdom motifs of its African religious roots is the language of the biblical texts, and the god-talk which it has influenced. The rhetoric associated with the Holy Bible has rightfully become the linguistic bridge.

Characteristics of African Religions

Familiarity with some of the general characteristics of African religions is essential to understanding the variety of traditions and how they are related. For instance, as I have said, many beliefs are common to all or most of the West African religions; but the beliefs were not propagated as such. Nor were missionaries sent to the neighboring "heathen" tribes, to preach the "better news." These very stable peoples simply and quietly assimilated ideas and practices from one another. However, the various religious systems themselves were closed, in the sense that they were coterminous with closed societies. Each nation or people had its own language, culture, and social, economic, and political order, as well as its own system of religion. One did and does not get converted to another system, nor does one seek to convert others. To do so would, as Mbiti declares,

involve propagating the entire life of the people concerned. Therefore a person has to be born in a particular society in order to assimilate the religious system of the society. . . . Those few Europeans who claim to have been "converted" to African religions . . . do not know what they are saying. To pour out libation or observe a few rituals like Africans, does not constitute conversion to traditional religions.[7]

African religions have neither founders nor reformers. They have neither "authorized versions" nor canonical scriptures. The religions simply flow out of the life of the peoples.

Another characteristic of African religions is the focus on the communal experiences of life—births and weddings, harvests and plantings, and funerals. The word celebration is appropriate to all these occasions, and the total community participates. In this sense, *every*body is religious and deeply familiar with the traditions. All are actively involved, although the tradition does not emphasize meditation and personal mysticism. Again, the serving of human needs is strong in the African cultures, but it is assigned to extended family and neighborhood ties. The obligation to help persons in need is supported indirectly by religious ideas of community as family but it does not involve consciously religious organizations and practices. There is also a great emphasis on religious objects and places. We shall deal later on with the whole African understanding of the spirit world, which is related to this.

Mbiti summarizes well the relationship between this African tradition and Christianity:

In matters of belief there are clear areas of common ground like God, continuation of life after death, spiritual beings, the works of God, etc. On these both Christianity and traditional religions overlap to a large extent. On the other hand, magic, witchcraft, sorcery and divination, which feature prominently in traditional religions, fall clearly outside the Christian orbit.[8]

Our description is further aided by Mbiti's delineation of areas which lie *between* Christianity and traditional religions, such as polygamy, a practice he holds to be neither condemned nor endorsed in the Bible, but which is used to deny full membership to many in African Christian churches which are dominated by missionaries.[9] He is quite right in pointing out a prevailing double standard. Men convicted of high crimes in government and business remain unchallenged as members in White Christian churches, while rigid rules still apply to the acceptance of Africans as Christian by overseas-oriented church traditions. The challenges in fully Christianizing any people are thus not at all unique to the African continent. As Mbiti evaluates the success of the much longer "Christianization" process in Euro-American civilization: "We all know that western civilization is not Christian, even though it does incorporate a lot of Christian influence in its long background and history."[10]

Whatever the mix of "good/Christian" and "bad/un-Christian" in African religions, it is at least exactly comparable to other religions of the world. And one need not hide the "lower" aspects in shame. In fact juju or conjure was often a merely inaccurate *science,* employed in the effective advancement of a good cause. The eminent psychiatrist Carl Jung had this to say about the freedom from rigid Catholic regulations which came to Europe with the Protestant Reformation: "A great amount of energy thus became liberated and went instantly into the old channels [pre-Christian European folk religion] of curiosity and acquisitiveness, by which Europe became the mother of dragons that devoured the greater part of the earth."[11] Compared to such an evaluation of the less-than Christian culture of Europe, the general characteristics of African traditional religions are humane and spiritual, to say the least.

Proverbs: Folk Wisdom and Faith

Before looking at some of the chief themes of West African traditional theology, or belief about God, a special look at the proverb source is necessary. The ideas contained in the proverbs were the original folk basis of the world view and of the rules of life of the African ancestors of Blackamericans. This form of oral literature is still tremendously important in West Africa today.

While the vast majority of proverbs have no obviously religious content, as Westerners view religion, an impressive theological tradition is evident in the small proportion which are intentionally "religious." The rest, although situationally oriented, are based on religious depth, reasoning, or world view and they are normative for behavior in the societies from which they come. The themes occur in massive similarity of motif, from Gabon and Eastern Nigeria's Iboland and Calabar, to Senegal on the West. My main emphasis is on the Yoruba and Ashanti in between, because of their larger populations, the greater availability of their folk literature in print, and their greater influence on Black culture in the Western Hemisphere.*

The oral tradition is still very strong among the Yoruba and Ashanti. Memory is regularly refreshed by drum recitation, dance, song, cultic reenactment, praise-speeches, stylized ritual insult (considered polite), and, above all, frequent use in conversation. The Yoruba declare that the proverb is the very "horse of conversation." The Ashanti hold, likewise, that "when the occasion comes, the proverb comes." Another Yoruba insight suggests that "A counselor who understands proverbs soon sets matters right."

The matter of translation into English of this oral literature is problematical. There is no "authorized" version of a folk tradition, any more than there can be an official version of a Negro spiritual. I have seen, in my own sources, as many as three versions of the same proverb in the original tongue. This variety of version produces variety of interpretation in subtle ways, serving only to complicate the already confusing implications. Compounding this difficulty is the gap between English and the African languages. Thus it becomes understandable why such a survey as *Black Belief* has not been attempted by more Black

---

*The selection of the proverbs used here has been greatly limited because of the fact that most of the publications available were produced for use as language-learning resources. The original writers or editors chose each proverb for its value as an example of elements of the language, as well as for popularity. These compilers, who were ministers in many cases, did not take the faith content of the proverbs seriously. They were not seeking to present a world view. Important religious ideas may therefore have been omitted from the sample proverbs available in print. However, the selection of proverbs used has been approved by African scholars as an accurately representative cross section.

The language-oriented sources of proverbs which are in print were dependent upon earlier collections, some dating as far back as the 1850s. African scholars themselves often depend on data gathered by Whites over one hundred years ago. So the need is established for the collection and publication of a better corpus of proverbs, from which someone may then develop a more comprehensive and perhaps more accurate survey of folk theology in West Africa.

scholars in America. Mbiti is the only African scholar to attempt a *religious* view of African folk beliefs.

Let us now look at some of the specific beliefs which occur in West African traditional religions.

Of Creation and the Fall of Man

The spiritual view of the world in West Africa is typically divided into four levels, described by Ezeanya as (1) Supreme or High God, (2) a vast hierarchy of lesser divinities and spirits, (3) ancestral spirits, and (4) evil spirits. However, while the world is not seen materialistically, this spiritual world is closely related to the material world. It is in the material world that the spirits display their powers, not elsewhere. Thus there is no basis in fact for the charge that African religion is otherworldly. Man has need of this spirit world, but African man fully assumes that the minor spirits have need of him, too, to gladden their hearts and feed them with good things.[12] Spirits are of *this* world, as well as related to the transcendent High God.

African traditional religions consider High God to have created the earth or the world, but the process and the agency of creation vary. One Yoruba tradition holds that Olodumare (High God) delegated the furnishing of creation to Orishanla, who got thirsty before he reached the job and drank too much palm wine. He became inebriated and fell into a long sleep. So Oduduwa, the chief ancestor of the Yoruba, came down on a chain, took Orishanla's tools, and finished the work of creation.[13] There is some evidence of conflation, since Orishanla, for some, is still God's chief deputy for creation and executive functions, and receives worship as the most important divinity.[14] The delegation of power and authority to create is not unlike the Johannine concept of Christ as Logos or Word, by whom all things were made, "and without him was not anything made that was made."[15]

High God is also thought of as having made man. An Ashanti proverb widely paralleled in other folk religions says that "all

men are the offspring of God, no one is the offspring of Earth."[16]
The Fon and the Yoruba say he made man of clay. The Yoruba
have a name for God which means "the Owner of the best clay."[17]
The Ashanti believe that when the creation was finished, He also
provided for laws and customs to regulate human life.[18] They
also believe that the task was done in six days and that God
(Nyame) went away on the seventh to get away from the further
complaints of his subjects.[19] Comparable creation stories with
specific numbers of days are common in West Africa, with the
Yoruba holding that it was four days. They, thus, have cultic
observances on the fifth day.[20] I have seen market days and worship days divided up on as many as three different modules in the
same society in Nigeria, all the way from fifth-day worship to
seventeenth-day markets.

The Ga of Accra are alleged to have been created by the widely
storied spider, who for doing so was brought to shame.[21] But the
most elaborate story of the Fall of Man, or the beginning of evil,
is a creation story coming from Calabar on Nigeria's east coast.
It was written down originally by a Scotch Presbyterian minister
named Hugh Goldie, in 1857. God sent man to earth to build fires
to warm Him and heaven, but man still ate in heaven. A woman
friend tempted him to strive for independence from God. Another woman, Abasi's (God's) wife, after convincing Abasi to
send man to earth and give him a wife, finally sent death to
punish man for becoming self-sufficient and defying God. Man
is guilty in the initiation of copulation with his wife, thus obtain-
ing the ability to create his own children.[22] It was a python (ser-
pent) who taught the first man and woman of one Ashanti sub-
group how to have offspring.[23]

The presence of evil in the world is blamed on a woman in a
fashion typical of Genesis in a widely known Ashanti myth.
Onyankopon (He who alone is great) ceased to live on earth or
very near to man because an old woman pounded fufu (mashed
coarse yam) too vigorously and hit him too often in the eye.[24] The
deity withdrew in anger and pain from the Eden-type existence
with man. Although it is God who leaves the garden and not man,

the features are interestingly related.

The sequel to the Ashanti story about the alienation of man from God is a myth about the same old woman trying to get back near God by building a tower of pestles (for pounding fufu). She almost succeeds, but, like the Tower of Babel, her tower collapses just before completion.[25] Above the Ashanti, and still in the slave zone, live the Dogon, whose beginnings go back to a demigod named Nommo. He descended to earth in an ark, with eight ancestors and and a supply of animals and plants, remarkably similar to Noah and his ark.[26]

Still another Ashanti myth tells how Tano, like Jacob, deceived his blind father, and obtained his older brother's inheritance. The older brother, Bia, was then forced to make do with the arid stretches of the Ivory Coast, while Tano received the rich inheritance of Ghana. This has geopolitical implications comparable to the assignment of Esau to the desert wastes of Seir and Edom.[27] A final example of material comparable to the biblical account of Creation comes from the Bambara, also north of the Ashanti. The Bambara celebrate the god of growth and nature every year, with a special feast every seventh year, much like a jubilee year. The recurrence of themes is not easily dismissed as accidental.

It is likely that the two strands of religious tradition making up Black folk belief go back to a primeval source out of which grew *all* mankind and many of his first beliefs. Certainly none of the gods, prophets or founders of "Western religions" actually came from Europe. Nor did any of their creation myths, flood stories and the like. They all come from Africa and Asia, with the African origins and influences well validated.[28] Africa, via Egypt, had crucial early influence on Greece and on the Hebrew religion. Once this is allowed proper weight it is not hard to see how beliefs in West Africa itself would have an even more likely common source to explain their widespread similarities. And, no doubt, the consciousness of a "fall of man" which slaves encountered in American English was traceable to the same sources as their own "fall"—deep in the early religious consciousness of human beings, on the African continent.

High God and the Many

The West African idea of God is a broad topic indeed. But all over the area, as in the mother's home in the play *Raisin in the Sun, there is God,* and the ideas about him are quite highly developed. We shall look closely at the two largest and most accessible cultures, the Ashanti and the Yoruba. While their ancestors did more selling than becoming slaves, the culture of the actual slaves was closely related.

Adebayo Adesanya, a Yoruba scholar, says that Yoruba myths were preceded by profound concentration and "in fact were a device to teach the generality of men to understand pictorially what they could not comprehend conceptually." He further states that "when one approaches an Ifa [divination] professor, one sees the entire absence of myth and one is carried to the realm of pure thought. . . . Myths allowed the Yorubas, I think, to achieve the architectonic," a design for making sense of human existence.[29]

The Yoruba tendency to narrow the creation of man down to their hometown, and to trace kings from each town directly to High God was their way of making, in each new town, a fresh, optimistic historic beginning. It was never an attempt to limit reality, but to narrow it down to a range comprehensible to the human mind.

It should not be unexpected that early White observers would be amazed at the profound culture and religion of African communities. In 1852, Samuel Crowther, a Yoruba, published a grammar containing an introduction by Anglican Bishop Vidal which included the following commentary by the Bishop. Yoruba proverbs have

a decidedly moral tendency. . . . [Proverbs] conduct men, not by circuitous argument, but immediately to the approbation and practice of integrity and virtue. They are everywhere in the mouths of all, . . . marking out a people of more than ordinary shrewdness, intelligence, and discernment. [They have brevity and elegance.] The poetry of the Yorubas, if I may call it such . . . remind[s] us, both in sentiment and style, of some of the poetical books of Scripture.[30]

In 1914, R. S. Rattray, an English civil servant and anthropologist who assumed a Christian monopoly on monotheism, wrote in his collection of Ashanti proverbs a similarly high appraisal of their concepts of God. He showed even greater amazement at the level of African independent theological development.

Untouched by European and Christian influence, it would seem incredible that the Christian idea of a one and supreme Being should . . . have taken such deep root as to affect their folklore, traditions, customs, and the very sayings and proverbs with which their language abounds. . . . References to a Supreme Being are far more commonly known among the greybeards, elders, and the fetish priestly class themselves than among the rising younger generation, grown up among new influences and often trained in the very precincts of a mission.[31]

Whatever may be said about the multiplicity of subdivinities, the fact remains that a form of monotheism is widespread in West Africa, and existed long before the first Europeans arrived. The following praise-names for God illustrate the Ashanti folk understanding of the deity in a very concrete way:

Onyame, Nyame. He who fills the sky, or the shining One.

Onyankopon. He who alone is great.

Odomankoma. God as absolute being, the architect and inventor, the Creator.

Brekyirihunuade. He who knows or sees all, before and behind, the Omniscient.

Totrobonsu. He who causes rain to fall copiously. The generous and magnanimous.

Abommubuwafre. Call upon in distress, a strong name.

Tetekwaframoa. He who endures forever and is of old.

Nyaamanekose. He in whom you confide troubles.

Onyankopon Kwame. That Onyankopon who came into existence on Saturday, the great ancestor whose day is Saturday.

Tweauampon. One on whom you lean (a tree) and don't fall.
Obooade, Boadee. The Creator.
Otumfo. Power, or to be able. He of power.
Amaonee. Giver of repletion, abundant satisfier of need.
Amosu. Giver of rain.
Amowia. Giver of sun.
Kokoroko. That which is great. Used of God in folk tales, along with Ananse the spider.[32]

These names have been drawn from Danquah and Rattray, but it is only fair to say that there is serious challenge of the validity of any interpretations which imply friendship with the deity and the possibility of direct dependence on him. There is also serious challenge by recent scholars of the tendency of Danquah and others to make the first three listed important names or aspects into a kind of trinity.[33] The multiplicity of praise-names does, however, imply a deep awareness of the inadequacy of a single name or idea to describe God. In addition the list follows the very common custom of praise, which applies also to speech to and about important or elderly people.

The Yoruba have a similar series of names for High God and a variety of interpretations as to meaning and importance. A most impressive folk phenomenon is Yoruba drivers who paint praise-names for God and religious sayings on the fronts and backs of their buses, trucks, and jitneys. Some use Christian (or at least English) names, and some use Islamic names, but many still use the Yoruba names in the bumper-to-bumper grind of the traffic snarls in Lagos and Ibadan. Here are the more important names:

Olorun. Owner (lord, chief, or ruler) of Heaven.
Olodumare. The Almighty. God the all-powerful.
Olofin Aiye, Oluwa (Aiye). Lord or ruler of earth.
Eleda. Creator, or owner of creation.
Alagi. The living One.
Elemi. Owner of spirit, Owner of the breath.
Alanu. The merciful God.
Olore. The Benefactor, the Well-doer.

Adakedajo. The silent active Judge.

Oyigiyigi Ota Aiku. The mighty, immovable rock that never dies.

Oba-Orun. King who dwells in heavens. (*Olorun* is a form of *Olofin-Orun,* Lord of Heaven.)

Olorun nikan 1' o qbon. Only Olorun is wise. (A saying.)[34]

The theological understanding of these names, if not taken too literally gives a fairly good sample of West African folk belief. It requires what, from a Western perspective, would appear to be a high tolerance for ambiguity, enigma, paradox, and contradiction. Actually, as mentioned earlier, it is a problem of subtlety and translation. For instance, Yoruba High God, Olorun, is utterly transcendent and ineffable, far beyond Christian ideas of transcendence. But the heaven he presides over is not made desirable by the implied distance from earth. The Yoruba believe their dead come back via reincarnation just as soon as they possibly can. Thus there evolves from this transcendence a very this-worldly religion.

As we shall see, God's inaccessibility is not held everywhere in West Africa, but it is generally accepted. The result is a focus on earth and life and power. The hierarchy of created lesser divinities (*orishas* in Yoruba, of whom Orishanla is chief) are expressions of this unreachable God, who is not person but vital power or energy. His lordship or authority stems, then, from a very earthy kind of consideration, *power.* The cult or worship of orishas, by whatever name, is designed to plug into that power, like electricity. The orishas are links to that power, although they seem to bestow their gifts independently of High God, limited only by their standing in the order of divinities and the specialty and territory, great or small which is their "jurisdiction."[35] In a sense ancestors are also spiritual beings, but their standing has a permanence not given to the others. The lower divinities, often residents of specific shrines (with priests) or other objects such as rivers or trees, are virtually discarded or abandoned when they fail to deliver. A believer may even change from the cult of one greater divinity to another, as we change our denominations in response to our needs. The focus on power is very pragmatic.

There are also evil spirits, but the Yoruba divinity, Eshu, is not completely evil. Words like messenger, prankster, and tester also fit him. He is a minister of God, according to Idowu, as Satan is in the Book of Job.[36] Nevertheless, Eshu, like all the other semi-evil spirits of West African religions, is dreaded. Of the evil spirits generally it may be said that their domain shrinks as obvious evils are eliminated by such things as hygiene and medical care, a process aided by expanded programs of education.[37] However, the demonic domain may also be increased for some by the unmanageable urban problems of housing and employment.

In most areas, where the inaccessibility of High God is deeply believed, there are no temples built in his honor and no priests ordained for his special service. Nor are any sacrifices offered. He would have no use for such. An interesting parallel to this concept is stated by no less a Christian authority than the Apostle Paul. The occasion was his attempt to reach the Greek intellectuals in the speech on Mars Hill in Athens: "God . . . seeing that he is Lord of heaven and earth [over other heavenly beings], dwelleth not in temples made with hands; neither is worshipped with men's hands, as though he needed anything."[38]

The fact that High God needs no priests or temples, however, seems only to exaggerate the need for priests to deal with the multiplicity of lower or intermediating divinities, as well as human problems. The tradition of Yoruba priesthood has thus developed to a very high level. The priestly role involves not only dealings with lesser divinities, but even more directly, dealings with such this-worldly needs as an herbal prescription for an illness. The three years of training required for the higher level and more stable priesthoods is quite professional from the Yoruba outlook. The Nigerian psychiatrist T. E. Lambo has employed priests in his in-culture therapy, using villages as alternatives to Western-style mental hospitals. The result has been far quicker cures at far lower costs.[39] The tremendous importance of conjure men and voodoo priests among the early American slaves is quite understandable in light of the effectiveness of their counterparts in West Africa this very day. "Only the *capable* priest gets the votive offering."[40] With God so far removed, good priests are widely needed.

There are some exceptions to the generalization about the inaccessibility of West African gods, however, and they must be mentioned here. The report of a conference on "The High God in Africa," held at the Institute of African Studies, University of Ibadan, in 1965,

did much to demolish certain hoary generalizations about notions of the supreme being in traditional African religion. For a start, the old assumption about an 'otiose' being with no cult [worship] took a hard knock. Ezeanya's paper brought up fresh material showing a highly developed cult of the supreme being in parts of Ibo country. . . . Baeta's paper also drew attention to the presence of a developed cult among the Akan. [Ashanti are the largest of the Akan group.][41]

At a January 1966 conference at Immanuel College (Seminary) in Ibadan, shortly after the one above, Ezeanya vividly describes the Ibo cult. When the insulting suggestion was made that the Ibo high priest might have borrowed his ideas about the High God from Christians he responded, "God has been among us from time immemorial; we weave sacrificial boat for him."[42]

The other generalization challenged at the conference had to do with God as underwriter of the moral order, but the informant was from East Africa. I am not aware of any major religion of West Africa holding to any deviation from the idea of a moral God. Indeed, the proverbs to be presented later indicate the justice of God as perhaps the strongest single West African attribute of God and/or his universe.

A final evidence of the accessibility of High God might be thought to be in spirit possession. This is the African parallel to the shouting evidence of God's presence in Blackamerican churches. Washington aptly states that "the heart of traditional African religions is the emotional experience of being filled with the power of the spiritual universe."[43] However, the weight of both evidence and reason would seem to support the opinion of

Beattie and Middleton regarding religions with no worship of the High God. "Spirit, in this most abstract sense, is not usually identified with any practically important aspect of social or physical environment, and there would therefore be little point in attempting to communicate directly with the High God. Contact is made with lesser spiritual forces . . . subordinate to but not identified with a single High God."[44] It is these lesser deities who possess the traditional religionist. While almost all of the peoples studied by Beattie and Middleton's writers believed in a High God, none, with the possible exception of the Yoruba, "thought that this God can enter into relationship with men through spirit mediumship." Spirit possession was later given great importance in relationship to High God among Blackamericans, as we shall see. But the beings who possessed persons in West African religion were and still are of a lesser order.

Sovereignty of God

While the heightened transcendence of High God common in West African religion precludes any coherent concept of his omnipresence, it certainly has not worked against his omnipotence and omniscience. Almighty Olodumare of the Yoruba is referred to as "Alewilese, He who alone can speak and accomplish His words"; and Olorun's face (implying the eyes) is the sky, seeing all that transpires. This omniscience is graphically portrayed in one Yoruba praise-name which means "He who sees both the inside and outside (of man), the Discerner of hearts."[45] The already mentioned Brekyirihunuade of the Ashanti also means the Omniscient. The Mpongwe of Gabon have a proverb which says "He knows the days before and He knows the days behind."[46]

Omnipotence is portrayed by proverbs as well as praise-names. In fact, there is a sizable corpus of folk wisdom which deals with the logical, living implications of the sovereignty and omnipotence of God. The most obvious implications of sovereignty have to do with the limits on the lesser divinities, and the limits on man in predestination.

The outer boundaries of power and influence available through the lesser divinities are widely proclaimed on appropriate occasions. The critique of orisha priests is paralleled by the strict limits declared on the powers of orishas themselves. For instance, the orishas let their priests die like everybody else. "The witch-doctor [*sic,* for orisha priest or, better, priest-doctor] will die, the medical doctor will go to heaven, and the consultant will not be left behind." [Yoruba]

No amount of charms can stop death. "Quantity has nothing to do with *juju;* battle kills the man with 1,400 medicine calabashes." [Yoruba] "It is when death has *not* come to a patient that *aja* [juju] on his neck is effective, but when he is actually due to die [destined], the aja will become useless and death will take away the life of the patient even with aja on his neck." [Yoruba] "Even the witch is in sorrow when her child dies." [Ashanti]

Christians say that God does not show partiality, sending his rain on the just and the unjust. The Yoruba say, "The rain does not recognize a person of honor; if the rain recognized persons of honor, it would not beat upon the worshipers of *Sango* and *Oya.*" Since parties to both sides of a controversy have alliances with lesser deities through their priests, the Ashanti know that "whichever side [wins] the die falls, we get a priest to hang."

There is no substitute for being careful and industrious in African religion. "The monkey says, 'My talisman [*suman,* lowest divinity] (against surprise and enemies) is my little eyes.'" [Ashanti] "There are no gods who support a man in his laziness; a man's greatest support is his own arm." [Yoruba] If the man means well and works hard, however, superstition does not hamper him either. "The soul of the man who would make good taboos nothing." [Ashanti]

There is also no African religious substitute for good character. "If you have magic charms and you are a gossip, the charms will not be effective." [Yoruba] "One must watch one's conduct and thoughts because when one asks the Ifa Oracle, it is going to answer according to thoughts in one's mind; it is necessary to realize that faith and character are the most important things in religion." [Yoruba; free translation.]

The proverbial wisdom against overdependence on the divinities believed to inhabit charms and the like is massive. Danquah translates an Ashanti saying to read that "the word of the elder is more potent than fetish." And Rattray has it, "The advice [literally "the mouth"] of a man of ripe years is more potent than (your) little guardian deity." The Yoruba offer a variation on the same theme, warning that "it is better to be bold than to be dependent on magic medicines." An understanding of the ultimate sovereignty of God underlies all this wisdom. It surfaces most explicitly in the sizable literature on predestination.

While the modern American mind tends to be repelled by such an idea as predestination, it must be remembered that African and original European Calvinistic doctrines were developed in a setting quite different from ours, with considerably different frames of reference. It is not necessary to comment at length on some of the modern caricatures made of Calvin's thought. Suffice it to say that the use of the term predestination in reference to African folk wisdom must not be understood to denote a straitjacket in which persons are irrevocably designated to spend eternity in heaven or hell. For Africans it means even more than the omnipotence of God recognized in a humble and realistic refusal to declare that man has final power. It means a positive declaration that reality is not random but under wise, adequately powered, divine control.

In a world view of vibrant affirmation of life, God's final authority underwrites and guarantees the evaluation of existence as good. Predestination is not an encroachment on man's freedom but a protection at the pragmatic periphery of man's powers to act. No man exercises absolute liberty, and those who accept their real limitations increase their enjoyment of the human journey. West Africans do not use the doctrine in advance as an excuse for inactivity, but often in retrospect as a guard against the horrible suspicion that life has no ultimate meaning. Given the additional African understanding of God's goodness (providence) and justice, predestination is celebrated as an integral part of man's reasonable fulfillment.

Here are a few of the proverbs related to predestination: "The destiny the Supreme Being has assigned to you cannot be avoided." [Ashanti] "The order God has settled living man cannot subvert." [Ashanti] "Abasi [God] sends you to market; when you have made your market, you must lift your basket and off." [Efik, of old Calabar, Nigerian coast, where all the world's a market.] "Unless you die of Onyankopon, let living man kill you, and you will not perish."

Christians say that man proposes and God disposes. African traditions say the same thing. "Things which they think, God does not think them (likewise)." [Gonja, Northern Ghana] "He who tries to shake a tree stump shakes himself." [Yoruba, saying for one who tries to oppose the inevitable.] "If God agrees, it will be done." [Gonja equivalent of the common Black precondition, "The Lord willing."]

West African predestination does not imply that all will be easy, but it teaches thanks to God for all stations in life: "However God places . . ." On the other hand, God's sovereignty guarantees that one need not overwork to obtain life's necessities. "Something we can do without rushing should not be done as if there were not enough time to do it; eventually everything will come to our hands. [Yoruba]

The fate assigned by God requires respect for the differences in others, as well as full acceptance of the obligations that pertain to one's own role. "The Lord of Heaven has created us with different natures." [Yoruba] "A hunchback is never asked to stand upright." [Yoruba] "Let the slave realize that he is a slave; let the pawn [for debts] realize that he is a pawn and let the gentleman realize that he is a slave of the gods." [Yoruba] While the Yoruba interpretation of this latter proverb is directed to making the rich serve others, the implications of a type of fatalism are inescapable.

It is possible, of course, to read African predestinarian belief as dumb resignation to whatever befalls—even slavery. Before arbitrarily denying the value of this interpretation, let us look at whatever strengths this view may have—the reasons why it has persisted so long and is still alive and doing well among some believers on both sides of the Atlantic. When one can celebrate life inside his supposedly divinely assigned role, no matter how low, it certainly reduces problems for all concerned. The Yoruba proverb says it quite frankly: "He who has been a slave from childhood does not know the value of rebellion (or slavery). Ironically, slavery is so completely taken for granted that the weight or use of the proverb is given by Delano, the Yoruba editor, thus: "He who has no experience of a thing cannot know its value and it is useless to ask him his opinion about it." This is typical Yoruba subtlety and an indirect, ritually coded statement. It is difficult to establish the need for social change in a society which is (as African society was at the time this ancient folk wisdom/-religion evolved) basically an extended family.

Slave status in Africa only indicated that one had lost a battle or couldn't pay a debt. One was therefore much more easily liberated from this slavery and/or added to the family than was ever true of monstrous American slavery. It is a paradox that among industrious people like West Africans, one is literally more free to be his best, ambitious self (exercising his options to escape his low estate) when he is inwardly content with "whatsoever state he is in," to use Paul's words.[47]

On the other hand, no Blackamerican should restrict his evaluation of African predestinarian world view to criteria involving a slavery so different that he will never really understand it. As logical as it may seem on the surface, it still presupposes a social stratification which is not acceptable to modern Black thinkers, African or American. A more penetrating analysis would yield not a directly opposite doctrine but a frank stripping away of any illusions whatever that one has arrived at a pat understanding of African world view. However, with a proper consideration of major parameters, one can arrive at a satisfying angle of vision.

The parameters, as I see them, are these:

1. *Destiny as Absolute.* This absolute is illustrated by the Ashanti proverb which says that no matter what you call him or how you plead, when death comes he will kill you.[48] What is true

of death is true of all of life. To try to change destined matters
is like trying to shake a great tree stump. You are the one who
"gets shook."

2. *Destiny vs. Activism.* In the Yoruba proverb which advises
against rushing, excessive activism is discouraged on the
grounds that reasonable exertion and the providence of God will
guarantee all one is due. "Everything will come to our hands."
This is much more of a warning against Western greed and acquisitiveness than a comfort to the lazy, who are abhorred all
over West Africa.

3. *Destiny vs. Charms.* The Yorubas state that "a person's destiny is more powerful than charms." There are many Yoruba
sayings about the fate one's *ori* ("head" or soul), kneels to receive
before God. It is sealed at the gate of heaven before the ori enters
a person via birth into the world.[49] The worship given the ori is
designed to keep it in good condition and to keep one on good
terms with it. But this is not expected to change one's destiny.

There is, nevertheless, complexity and paradox in actual practice. An elusive combination of acts and agents exist whereby a
Yoruba's destiny may undergo change: (a) By aid of *Orunmila*
one may have a happy destiny preserved or an unhappy one
rectified. (b) Not that Olodumare has any evil in him, but he did
create evil spirits. The problem of why and for what purposes
these spirits exist is never raised. (c) Bad character and acts of
impatience or rashness can spoil or forfeit even a good destiny.
(d) In a kind of early detection process, the oracle is consulted the
third day after each birth to ascertain what kind of child it is,
what is taboo for it, and what is required to preserve its good
destiny or change its bad. This can be done also in later life in
crises. (e) Birth under the sign *Enikeji* requires special offerings
throughout life, if one is to thrive.

This rather complicated Yoruba system is not atypical of the
religions of West Africa. It is described here not only because of
the size and influence of the Yoruba religious tradition and its
resultant value as a sample, but because a detailed analysis in
print of African religions is uncommon. Few have been so well

preserved and are so well researched by African scholars, but all the West African traditions undoubtedly had a comparably broad spectrum of pragmatic approaches to destiny and charms, retaining the hopes and avoiding the excesses which would accrue to an overly literal and simple approach. At the more profound level of the oracles of Ifa, as over against the more superficial level of charms, the overall effect of the corpus is to give hope for the most deeply desired goals of all Africans—long life, with adequate means of support, and children to survive one and carry on one's name with honor.[50]

4. *Advice (Common Sense) vs. Charms.* As one moves along the spectrum, away from the rhetoric of the fixedness of ultimate destiny, one is wiser to seek advice from an elder than to use charms seeking the intervention of subdivinities. The Yoruba and Ashanti traditions unequivocally declare common-sense alternatives to be more potent than fetish.

5. *Charms vs. Change (the Uncertain).* With the arena of the unpredictable thus narrowed, the West African still acknowledges some shifts in the human condition as beyond both the scope of destiny and the expectation of reason. A Yoruba proverb says: "Things are not likely to be the same tomorrow as they are today; this is why the *babalawo* [Ifa priest] consults the Ifa Oracle every five days."[51]

One finds it necessary to seek help in those matters unrelated to destiny, as ascertained and corrected if necessary, and beyond the help of wise advice or common reason. But the pragmatic mind so prevalent in the culture knows that even the priest's prayers and revelations yield results in accordance with the seeker's character. One proverb wisely puts it that the oracle can answer only within the frame of reference of thoughts one already has in his mind.

Joseph R. Washington, Jr., in discussing African fatalism and the predestinarian influence on Blackamericans, suggests that "instead of doing nothing or resigning themselves to human powers and institutions which work against them, traditional black folk come together in community around the *cult* where they seek guidance for their common destiny."[52] This amounts to saying that the African beliefs and cult, to which Blackamericans turned in the crisis, were at best a subtly *non*fatalistic influence. An active decision was made to accept a *divine* determinism and seek a *divine* power, rather than to resign to hostile, demonic *human* powers. In fact, it is significant that even though Black folk believers in a supposed fatalism had quietly accepted African styles of slavery, they persistently denied any possibility that God had predestined the American style of slavery. This obstinate insistence on the goodness of God may appear to contradict predestination in a Western-oriented thought system, but it is quite at home with the African world view of God's justice.

Goodness and Providence of God

The goodness and providence of the Supreme Being are the opposite side of the coin of the sovereignty of God. No man can affirm the goodness of life, as Africans do, without the same affirmation of its Creator, whose goodness would be mere sentimentality if he didn't have the omnipotence to guarantee it. Providence, then, is the goodness of a powerful deity, implemented in the ultimate working of "everything together for good."[53] This phraseology from the Apostle Paul may seem odd in the African context, since one must still act in such a way as to please the created deities. However, it is well understood that the lesser divinities control the lesser details of life. The providence and justice of High God apply to the total direction of one's life. No lower-level spiritual being has the power to pervert justice in the long run.

Such a belief in ultimate providence is essential to the consistent affirmation of the goodness of life. No Western or other doubter can "prove" that Africans are wrong, since the belief constitutes a self-fulfilling prophecy. When things go well, the prophecy is justified. When life's joys are mixed with sorrow, one exercises selectivity in his focus on the facts, or else he engages in a survey, natural and supernatural, to see what he did wrong. In any case, his theory is still intact. Should life come to utter desolation (a rare possibility, given this view), one has still the option of aroused curiosity or long-standing myths, as to the way God makes all work out for good. Since in African culture dilemmas tend to be solved with time, there is no way ever to "prove" that the providence of God has finally failed. There is always more time to wait for a more positive reading.

There is also the body of proverbial tradition which warns that a good life actually *has* to have some grief and woe. One Yoruba proverb suggests that "if the farm were not hard to till, the blacksmith would not make hoes for sale." The Ashanti say that "if one eats the honey alone, it plagues his stomach." Also, "The lizard says, 'If ever man attained complete satisfaction he would go crazy.'" More direct is the Yoruba proverb which declares, "When the skin is not hurt, it says that it has no flesh (to protect it)." This suggests that when circumstances do not call forth a man's resources, he is apt to think he has none.

These attitudes are profound and reasonable in an earth-wise, positive people. Their track record in the African experience, and in American slavery and oppression, forces the most extreme cynic to take a second look. Already beyond philosophical proof or disproof, the pragmatic value of belief in providence is that it keeps the believer's hopes, and with them his creativity, alive. His provident world view frees him to focus his awareness not only on the rewarding aspects of existence but on the greatest responsibilities as well. Rather than blissful ignorance, this view is the affirmation and celebration of life as a whole so characteristic of West Africa and so needed in the spiritually barren wastes of other continents. It is a bit ironical that Ezeanya can declare the doctrine of the providence of God to be so strong in Ibo (Eastern Nigerian) traditional religion today, that Christian missionary "teaching on divine providence . . . will surely appeal to the Igbo [Ibo]."[54]

The goodness of creation and the Creator are so taken for

granted that there are few sayings so direct as the Ashanti proverb: "The hawk (poised aloft) says, 'All things the Supreme Being made are beautiful (good).'" There are many aspects of the broader principles of goodness and providence. Thus, "A good spirit looks after its child." [Ashanti]

The theme expressed in the spiritual, "I'm so glad, trouble don't last always," is expressed: "The Aro does not always bear its load: it will put down sooner or later." The Aro holds pots over a fire. This Yoruba saying is consolatory. "Things at worst will surely mend." The Gonja of northern Ghana put the same thing in the form of a question: "What war comes and does not end?" With equal concreteness the Yoruba declare that "the eyes may be red and yet not blind; the banana may look ripe and yet not be soft; the trouble which causes so much anxiety will be overcome. It will not kill one."

Providence as protection from evil, or as the undoing of its results is also declared proverbially. "Leave the battle to God, and rest your head (or temple) upon your hand (as spectator). This is the Yoruba equivalent for the biblical theme of "Vengeance is mine; I will repay, saith the Lord."[55] "Man beats the drum of slander for the people's downfall, only God Almighty will not let it sound." [Yoruba] There is beauty as well as faith in the Ashanti belief that "when the Supreme Being fills your gourd cup full of wine and a human being comes and pours it away, He will fill it up again for you." For the Gonja, the providence of God delivers even from perils common to the modern city: "If they tie my arms and my legs, how am I to loose them? God will loose them."

Then there is a group of providential proverbs which declare that God also compensates for those problems in which he may have had a causative hand. The imagery rises to moving, poetic heights, as seen in this Ashanti saying: "If the Supreme Being gives you sickness, He (also) gives you medicine." To poetry is added ingenuity in Gonja belief. "God arranges things so that a leper's sandal breaks under the camelfoot shrub (which provides the rope to mend it)." West Africans portray confidence in God's care most impressively, with a variety of figures. "It is God who drives away the flies for the cow who has no tail."[56] [Yoruba, Anga, and others] It is the Supreme Being who pounds *fufu* [like mashing hard potatoes] for the one without arms. [Ashanti]

A kind of personal care, despite the transcendence of God, is seen in the preceding series. Other proverbs imply that fatherly relations, divine guidance and vocation, and outright grace are part of the providence: "All men are children of the Supreme Being (Onyame); no one is a child of the earth." [Ashanti] "Things are never so bad that there remains nobody at our side, but we do not know who it is will remain." [Yoruba] "The needle says that it is not because the iron is finished that I was made small; I am made for a purpose." [Gonja] "If God should compute our sins, we should perish." [Yoruba]

Bowen, who wrote in 1858 as a Southern Baptist missionary, heard this last proverb used to help settle disputes, and suspected it was borrowed from the Moslems.[57] This may be simply one inability to concede the high level of African religion. On the other hand, if his view is true, the open-mindedness of the Yoruba and their good judgment in using such would detract not a whit from the impressiveness of their religion. And if their overall view, emphasized the ineffability or transcendence of God, they were in exactly the same position as the Old Testament Hebrews. In both cultures and traditional religions, there was also a strong and socially relevant understanding of the justice and/or righteousness of God.

Righteousness and Justice of God

The common White stereotypes of West African religion and Western hemisphere voodoo tend to assume a fickle, perverse, and even perfidious deity, whose aid may at times be enlisted in petty personal vendettas. This is grossly in error. A good example of a more typical invocation of divine intervention is Ezeanya's Ibo, who asks Supreme God to use *His* thunder to signal *His* righteous verdict in a dispute between parties.[58] There is, perhaps, no larger body of sayings than those related to the justice of God. It is certain that no belief has more importance for the social good.

The folk doctrine is both implicit and explicit. For example, the Calabar saying, "The controversy (or displeasure) of God follows the sin of man" implies a God who is himself good and just, and whose commands and demands are manifestly consistent with both his own nature and the human good. His principles are woven into the very structure of the universe and its preeminently spiritual processes. Idowu says of the Yoruba High God that "man is in the hands of the Deity whose dictate is law, and who is waiting on the other side of this life to render to him as he deserves."[59]

This just God also renders according to what a man deserves right here in this world. There are many rough equivalents of the Bible text so popular among Blackamericans: "Be not deceived; God is not mocked: for whatsoever a man soweth, that shall he also reap."[60] The immutability of justice is literally celebrated as a part of the goodness of life. It is joyously anticipated rather than feared. One Yoruba proverb-prayer voices the visceral petition that "death not kill the man who tortures us, may the gods protect the man who ill-treats us; however long it may be before our destiny will give us victory." There is no question whatever about the wrongdoer's punishment. The prayer is simply for the privilege of seeing the divine retribution in this life, rather than knowing that "he got his" in the next.

One sees a certain corporate genius in the number of facets of the justice of God with which the Yoruba child is bombarded. There is the sowing and reaping facet. "To sow is difficult, to reap is free; what you sow today is what you reap tomorrow." The sowing is not all visible; one also sows and develops character. "Character is a God; according to the way you behave it supports you." Hidden harm to others also returns, equally hidden. "If a man secretly betrays his friend, evil things will secretly happen to him." But most of it is out in the open. Evil attracts attention as flies are attracted to dung. "One who excretes in the road will find flies when he returns." Justice is not all retribution either. Good as well as evil returns. "The kindness we show to the hen is not lost, eventually it will make gravy in our mouth."

However, the negative seems easiest to portray and remember, even though the end result is the positive projection of a happily just and dependable universe. The Yoruba say that divine justice is as direct as the wind blowing ashes right back in your face. "The stone we throw up at the coconut, the coconut throws back at us." In fact and contrary to stereotypes of pervasive evil magic, West Africans generally teach that one can have no protection against the evil he unleashes in the world. "He cut a tree and fell over it himself." [Ga, Accra] There is a law that things unpleasing to God are drawn right back to their source. "The bat says he will ease himself to smear God but (the feces) will turn to smear himself." [Gonja] The return of ill will is as obvious as the fingers on your hand. "If you raise a finger against your companion, the remaining ones will bend to look at you." [Gonja]

The Yoruba say also that "the badness of the yam is (laid to) the badness of the knife: (but it is soon found out that the yam is in fault; so) he who injures another injures himself." This proverb teaches not only justice as retribution but justice as exposure. It embodies the popular wisdom that the truth will out, and the biblical guarantee that "there is nothing covered that shall not be revealed."[61] The succinct Gonja declaration is, "The time has come." This is understood by them to mean that the time will come when truth will be revealed and everything brought to light. It is the divine detective, as it were, who makes sure all the evidence gets to court, thus assuring the justice of God.

The variety of figures from earthy to lofty keeps the recurrence of the theme from being monotonous, but the point is always made. There can be no doubt that dishonesty is expected to be exposed from Senegal to Calabar, or throughout West Africa. "When they rot, they will smell." [Gonja] "Telling lies to have honour—disrespect is the end of it." [Yoruba] "Many destroy themselves with falsehood." [Calabar] "The headlong fall of a liar is not concealed, but is exposed to view." [Yoruba] "(As) the Ife people (the forefathers of the Yoruba) speak without disguise, (so) a poisoned arrow kills an animal in the sight of all." "Matters which cannot be hidden must remain in the open; when a horse dies it must be buried outside." [Yoruba] "Lies, however numerous, will be caught by truth when it rises up." [Wolof, Senegal]

Truth, here, is assigned a kind of personality, and it partakes of the omniscience of God, whose justice is not at all blind. The Gonja say it, "God knows if the bat is drinking water; God knows if it does not drink water." The symbolic blindness of justice is designed to avoid partiality, an objective achieved other ways. One we have already seen, in that the rain beats on honorable worshipers of Sango and Oya, in Yorubaland. They also say it, "As the Segge [tall, coarse grass] does not regard the king's messenger, so the rain does not respect great men." There is no question that West Africans believe in the same quality of the deity which is expressed in the Matthew account where Jesus says God "sendeth rain on the just and the unjust."[62]

Related to the inability to hide truth is the inability to hide character, and the great unlikelihood that it can be changed. The recurrent theme of the leopard's inability to change his spots is stated positively in the Dahomey Yoruba proverb, "Although a snake casts away beads and sheds its skin, it cannot change its color; nor can I my word." So the emphasis placed on the incurability of monkeys' squatting or pigs' wallowing in the mire is not a statement of flat fatalism but a warning of the difficulty of change. At the same time attention is constantly focused on the importance of character. Part of the very justice of God is the cumulative effect of the habits one chooses or acquiesces to, and one does not leave his habits at home, no matter how long the journey, as one Yoruba proverb says. The grim warning of the Gonja of Ghana is that "a crooked tree cannot be straightened." The Ashanti say that "though the goat determines to turn into a sheep, there will always be a patch of black somewhere." Since the change is so difficult and the justice so strict, the best way to handle character and habit is to start right.

A great deal of attention is devoted to the theme, therefore, of children being like their parents, with the warning that the parents should be the right kinds of patterns, or models. Children are very important in Africa, and every effort is usually made to rear children whose reputation will be a credit to their aging parents. Lest one forget his own character, and think he can improve the next generation, he hears that "the crab does not beget a bird. [Ga, Accra] "The child of an elephant will resemble his mother, the son born to an elephant will resemble an elephant." [Yoruba] "A sheep does not give birth to a goat." [Ashanti] Unmistakably, "The viper begets an adder, the cruel father begets a cruel child; we resemble our parents." [Yoruba] The folk belief of West Africans is thus inevitably brought around to practical life, and no discussion can evade the pragmatic or remain (if indeed it can start to be) theoretical.

Spiritual vs. the Material

In the West African view the material is subordinate to the spiritual. Two virtually identical key proverbs set the tone and theme, recalling the Old Testament idea that "man shall not live by bread alone."[63] The Yoruba advise, "Do not take your ten fingers to eat." In Ghana they say, "Though you are hungry, you do not eat with both hands." [Ashanti, Twi] This may seem to be table manners, but it is a way of saying that a man should never occupy his entire energies with the business of gaining material things, not even food.

Here is a series of related comparisons and other maxims. The meaning is clearly that extreme materialism has many practical pitfalls. "A (good) name is better than eating (i.e. possessing)," and, "To own a *few* things is better than to be a thief." [Gonja] When one cannot be content with what he has, he becomes covetous, which leads to much worse sins. "When what *you* have is not good, you do not go and take what belongs to someone else." "When you admire something belonging to another, go get your own, do not steal it." [Ashanti] A subtle Yoruba saying really means that covetous people are unfit for society. "As the envious man has nothing, so grass matting is unfit for trousers." Also, "Covetousness is the father of disease." Africans have their own equivalent to the European fable about the goose that laid the golden egg. "A tree belonging to an avaricious man, bore abundantly; but instead of gathering the fruit (little by little), he took an axe and cut it down (that he might get it all at once)." Materialists are likened to flies. "The fly heeds not death, eating is all to him." [Yoruba]

West Africans are not dualists, but they are spiritually aware of the ephemeral nature of material things. Their ways of expressing this are varied and profound. "Although you have many provisions, you will see the end of them." [Wolof, Senegal] "Inordinate gain makes a hole in the pocket." [Yoruba] "Death has the key to open the miser's chest." [Ashanti] So one ought to live well and take care to enjoy life instead of trying to build a big estate. "The world is not all full of enjoyment; therefore the day a little pleasant thing comes your way, enjoy it; the day many pleasant things come your way, enjoy them; when an elder falls down the contents of his stomach will not be thrown out of him; what you eat goes with you (to the grave)." [Yoruba]

This kind of balanced evaluation of life is also shown in something of an opposite situation, in a rare example of the spiritual in isolation from the material: "If you have no money (to give to one in distress), you may pay frequent visits; if you cannot visit, you may send good words of the mouth (i.e., kind messages)." [Yoruba]

The tradition of mutual assistance is very strong in West Africa, and the implication of many proverbs is that kindness and love are indispensable. The community is, after all, an extended family, and the fact that it is so spiritual is not at all self-conscious or pious. The Gonja describe the supportive relationship in a sound and unforgettable way. "Take your beloved one and throw him (to) stand (on his) feet." Sharing or generosity is in the very nature of things. The Ashanti express this inevitability by reminding all that "it is one man who kills an elephant, but many people who eat its flesh." Sharing is also implicit in the great tradition of hospitality, without which, until recent years, travel would have been impossible. The Ashanti proverb for it is picturesque and pointed: "When the porcupine is going to visit the porcupine, he does not take any food with him."

When the man with the handicap of a withered hand was declared to be in charge at the gate of the gods, there was no noblesse oblige or patronizing. *All* men have to be helped at times. "Assisting me in putting my load down [perhaps from the head] is the same service another person has rendered to me. (One gives in return for what one receives.)" [Gonja] "When the right hand washes the left, and the left hand washes the right, then both hands will be clean." [Yoruba and many other cultures]

The idea of love as such is seldom mentioned, but the few examples one can find go straight to the heart of the matter. "Hate is no medicine." [Ga, Accra] "He who does not love his neighbor acts maliciously." [Yoruba]

The idea of formal religion is likewise almost never mentioned in connection with these mutual obligations. Here is just one: "The cult member supports the arm (elbow) of his fellow member; if one member does not support another member, the cult will be disgraced." [Yoruba]

Acceptance/Permissiveness and Peace

The African affirmation of life requires, in addition to this mutually supportive love, a deep respect for human personality. Otherwise the only life affirmed would be one's own. This respect is expressed in a kind of awe before each destined-to-be unique personality—a shyness about meddling with or trying to control another. One not only celebrates the spontaneous creativity and fulfillment of another (such as is encouraged in jazz and gospel improvisation), one actually recognizes the right of another to make his own mistakes. Some have viewed this as overpermissiveness, spoiling (almost worshiping) of children, and even as just plain indolence—laziness "begotten by the tropical sun." However, to see this accepting spirit *with* an accepting spirit and mind is to wish that all cultures might so love and spoil their children. Every community ought to be filled with such peaceful nonintervening persons—"deficient" in the personal power lusts that are so characteristic of many societies.

To be sure, even before the plague of Western influence, the admonitions of the proverbs were not followed literally. These proverbs are the precepts of the wise and the good segment of society. But they were the normative goals of all of the West African societies, and a pervasive sense of disrespect for these rules has yet to emerge. The man who properly understands and observes this set of sage sayings will have a head start towards successful child rearing, and the nation that takes the sayings seriously will be well on its way to peace.

The themes are not strange to American or Western or Christian ears. They run the gamut from the Blackamerican popular hit that declares "It's *your* thing," to the New Testament pattern for peace which suggests that if some aggressive person takes away your cloak, you ought not to oppose his taking your coat also.[64] Such wisdom is contrary to American culture, whereas in African it is on the lips of hundreds of thousands of people, particularly the proverb-loving folk pundits of West Africa.

The laws of African life are not followed in self-conscious "goodness" or piety. They are more a matter of awareness of mutual vulnerability to error, and mutual need to be free, as well as to be open for the benefits that accrue because of good relationships between people. "We can see the backs of other people's heads, and other people can see the back of ours." [Yoruba]

Interdependence is such that one cannot hold others back without limiting himself. The Gonja and others say that "if you don't allow your companion to cut nine, you will not cut ten."

This emphasis on pragmatism is seen again and again. The Yoruba say that "if you *appreciate* kindness shown to you, you will receive *more* kindness." For the Yoruba, there is the simple judgment that "anger does not accomplish anything; patience is the chief virtue." An earlier version of the same proverb has it: "Anger does nobody good; patience is the father of dispositions. Anger draws arrows from the quiver; good words draw Kola nuts (presents) from the bag."

The positive view of creation and Creator, as seen in nature, supports the idea of permissiveness with pragmatic parables. "If the hawk does not want to tease the kite the sky is big enough for any number of birds to fly without bumping into each other." This Yoruba saying means that when a man in a superior position is finding fault with a subordinate, he is often fabricating an excuse for punishing or disgracing him so as to show his power and satisfy his ego. But the world is too big for people to have to hurt others to help themselves. "The hen knows when the dawn comes, but she nevertheless looks to the cock (to make it known)." [Ashanti] Hens have other ways to express their talent and draw attention.

Permissiveness is advocated in practical specifics. "When a person says that he will climb up the tree stump (whose boughs have been cut off), let him climb; he will go to the face (the top), and return." [Ashanti] Another version of the same parable relates it to children. "When a child says he is going to climb the stump of a tree, let him climb (it), for when he has gone up it (a little way) he will turn back again."

Several other proverbs deal with children in the same vein. "If a child insists on handling a live coal, let him; he will throw it away when it burns him." [Ashanti] " 'Be like me, be like me'; these words make one a hard master." So Yoruba parents are advised to allow their children to follow their natural bent. The Gonja say that a father can only advise a son; he cannot prevent him from doing evil. "It is only your ulcer that I am cleaning, I am not going to apply medicine to it."

Lest the impression be given that West African cultures are anarchically loose-leaf, there are well-stated proverbs of moderation. The Gonja advise one to deal moderately with persons, not too hard and not too soft. "The Kantimanto drum says, 'I am the chicken egg's drum; if you beat me a little, I will not sound; if you beat me more, I break.' " Contrary to slave-master theory, West Africans do not love or encourage tyrants. Yoruba and Ashanti kings who became tyrants were advised to commit suicide to avoid being murdered. It was an offer they could not refuse.

The Gonja also suggest that one listen to both sides of a case before giving judgment. "They do not praise a race with a single horse." The justice implied here is common. Human beings reflect the justice ascribed to their High God. "Do not receive a slander against any one to accuse him falsely." [Yoruba] "Do not reject the case of the mahogany because he is bitter."[65] This is an Anga (northern central Nigeria) admonition against prejudging a person already known to be wicked or bitter like the mahogany. As in the United States, a man should be presumed innocent until proven guilty.

Anyone who has ever seen a good West African argument will know that the permissiveness and care for persons' rights are not antithetical to the facing of truth, either. The Yoruba believe that the best way to friendship that lasts is to question things one does not understand. They put it quite bluntly. " 'Offend me and I'll question you' is the medicine for friendship." Neverless, the Yoruba also suggest that "strife never begets a gentle child"; and "an affair which we conduct with gentleness is not marred; an affair which we conduct with violence causes us vexation."

There is also the awareness that, at times, "discretion is the better part of valor." So the Wolof of Senegal advise, "If the bull would throw thee, lie down"; and the Yoruba suggest that "if a great (or powerful) man should wrong you, smile upon him." Throughout it all, the goal is peace, and the Yoruba compare a peacemaker to velvet, which finishes a dress like the right proverbs finish a dispute.

The pragmatic value of this collection of proverbs on permissiveness is self-evident. However, the divine dimension, like the love and cult seldom mentioned, is unquestionably present. "The Lord of Heaven has created us with different natures." [Yoruba] I can only wish that the West African tradition on this and other topics were much better known among Blackamericans, and that their own Black Christianity were so accurately and casually remembered and practiced.

I have disavowed any attempt to do a West African "summa theologica," but it has been manifest time and again that the ethics which grow out of the celebration of God and life are a very coherent system within themselves. It is hard to find a set of African pure abstractions, and the attempts at the folk level have ended in the kinds of difficulty one sees in the attempt here to establish the parameter "Destiny vs. Charms." That Africans do think quite profoundly and conceptually where it really counts is evident however. At the risk of redundance, may I say again that this level is in practical living. It is at this same level that I shall try to describe the corpus of Blackamerican folk belief. By now it goes without saying that I consider the roots of the beliefs portrayed in this chapter to derive more from the substance and emphasis of this African corpus than from the overlapping Christian corpus, the Bible, and the influence of the Christian White tradition. I consider that both traditions have been greatly enlarged and enriched by this confrontation or interface of cultures. To be a son of that creative confrontation and adaptation is a privilege inadequately appreciated by Blackamericans and even less by others.

FOUR

The Generation of Meaning
in Black America

In the early years, before the havoc of European contact and commerce, a Black faith or world view was quite accurately recorded in the minds of whole African communities. Their pre-Christian understanding of God was wonderfully supportive of life. This faith is now being lost, and it should be preserved in the original languages, by its true believers, before it erodes away completely in deadly confrontation with materialistically superior cultures. An Afro-American adaptation of and counterpart to this body of Black belief developed early in this country. If one assumes that it took from 1619 to 1815 to develop, it was for another half century a means of survival under slavery. It has upheld Blacks in unofficial wage slavery and injustice ever since Emancipation. Before it is lost through acculturation it also needs to be written and shared to continue the dynamic Black process of overcoming the hardness of life by means of a creative faith.

My approach is to deal with the theology of the Black masses, tracing their faith primarily through *spoken* accounts of their lives. The informants were mostly the nonliterate survivors of slavery. All the statements were delivered orally even when the subject could read and write. Many of their interviewers were White, and the standard questions, usually designed by a folklorist, reveal strong biases in support of folk stereotypes. But occasionally the facts of their faith shone through despite loaded questions. The majority of the material was gathered all over the South, mostly as a project of the Works Progress Administration, in the Depression; and the vastness of the corpus tends to provide adequate basis for uncovering the world view and faith which shows in and above and below the lines.

The corpus of slave autobiographies is subject to question from various perspectives. One suspicion stems from the implausible percentage of reports which say that maltreatment was all around, but *"my* massa' was *good* to *me."* Careful reflection forces one to lay the blame for the apparent selectivity of interviewers or dishonesty of ex-slaves at an interesting point: the life expectancy and death rate among the various kinds of slaves. Those who had managed to be alive seventy years after slavery were, for the most part, those who had been treated well. The gruesome fact is that heartless overdemand for work, malnourishment, and merciless beatings hardly allowed the maltreated to make it into the twentieth century at all. In fact, many brutalized contemporaries of those interviewed in the 1930s never even saw the close of the Civil War. Yet the deeper folk world view of the surviving ex-slaves would hardly have been expressed in terms not common to all of the slaves. There is certainly no *more* reliable source than their hundreds of testimonies about their lives. This is true even though one can see them occasionally and obviously using the interview to plead with the interviewer for pensions and tips, out of sheer hunger.

It is a searching commentary on the economic system that those who survived and took on the dependency roles of "house nigger" should suffer such deprivation. It is a judgment on the whole society that those who worked so hard and faithfully should arrive at advanced old age penniless. If this irony had been more obvious to narrative project directors, they would no doubt have given less emphasis to the "gallant old days of the South," and the Blacks who fitted in, to their eventual undoing.[1]

There are still other challenges stemming from the fact that a majority of the biographees were children when they were slaves, and would remember their experience with childish fancy. On the other hand, one cannot deny that children are the best index to the world views of their parents, both in their verbal expressions and in their nonverbal exemplification of value systems. It is also true that I have compensated for this bias by assigning weight to cogent nonagenarians and centenarians in accordance with their maturity during slavery. Careful sifting for children's imagination also helps the accuracy of the evaluation of the material, but the introduction to the Fisk Collection mentions a concept called "realistic fabrication," which would give validity to children's creations from factual elements.[2]

The testimony of the ex-slaves includes and/or implies three written American sources of folk theology in addition to their frequent mention of the crucial and widely familiar "spirituals." The first source is their common quotation of biblical texts popular among slaves, a theological index at least as important as the spiritual songs, if not more so. A second source emerges in occasionally quoted and highly popular White hymns, which also reveal beliefs they held dear and appropriated. We shall see an excellent use of such at the close of the section on the grace of God. Then, thirdly, there are Black restatements of doctrines of White origin which are highly significant.

The biblical texts which gained popularity constituted an authentic *oral*-culture Hebrew and early Christian folk religion, captured in English and in print, which, on a highly selective basis, appealed to the slave. The inescapable use of English and the compatibility of biblical content with African tradition rendered the texts extremely accurate as indexes to early Black folk belief. As proverbs and religion had salted their speech in Africa, so this religious material was spread through their daily conversation. Ninety-seven-year-old Mack Taylor of South Carolina illustrates the point: "I have laid away four wives in deir graves. I have no notion of marryin' any more. Goodness and mercy have followed me all the days of my life, and I will soon take up dis old body and dwell in de house of de Lord forevermore."[3] As

African culture and religion had been stable, so also, once the slave had fashioned a faith for his condition and selected his favorite themes, did he maintain a rather stable folk religion here. There are, in fact, real trends towards recovery rather than major shifts away from the faith of the Black Fathers. And the use of biblical texts known to be popular is not only an aid to the sophisticated Black preacher who wants to plug into the powerful folk tradition, but an accurate window into the folk belief on which it is based.

While much of the slaves' religious experience was outside the scrutiny and influence of the masters, late at night, or *From Sundown to Sunup,*[4] there were times when, as in the appropriation of scriptural passages, White doctrinal statements *appealed* to slaves as useful inside their experience. When this occurred, they boldly and typically took unto themselves doctrines, casually sharing their strengths in ever-widening circles of open Black ears and minds. Eighty-eight-year-old George Briggs of South Carolina had obviously made such a useful selection when he declared: " 'Once in de Spirit, allus in de Spirit.' A child of your'n is allus a child of your'n. Dat de way de Baptist teach— once a child of God, allus God's child."[5] The utility of the doctrine of the perseverance of the saints is slanted towards needed acceptance in a hostile world, but it also comes in handy when one is about to take a great risk for liberation and is worried about pressures and possible loss of life or of sanity.

That slaves heard what they wished and tuned out what didn't serve their purposes is obvious through their voting, at times, with their feet, against what they were hearing. The extreme opposite of the above acceptance of a doctrine was seen in an ex-slave's scornful report of his master's doctrinal pretensions when he declared, "I am your only God," and had his "jack-leg" proclaim, "Honor your missus and your massa that your days may be long."[6] Slaves easily detected misuse of scripture and the denial of their humanity, and sought the will of God as opposed to the will of the most powerful of men. Their sense of divine guidance turned up in virtually all the decisions of the devout, and was a consideration of major folk proportions almost everywhere. Whereas it had been more a matter of *appeasing* deities in Africa, it became in America more a matter of *pleasing* the Christian God, but the difference was more of degree than kind. And there was *no possible confusion of God with ol' massa.*

Whatever the masters' powers on this earth, God was, as clearly stated by so many Black theologians, the ultimate source of power. This was not theological theory but world view at the gut level—the intuitive certainty that the universe is in higher hands, and that they are benevolent. A former slave, painfully aware that in his master's mind he had not been considered even to have a mind or soul, stated it simply: "Oh where else can we go but to the Lord."[7]

It may be successfully argued that this Lord in America was powerful all right, but he was also still White. Slave visions of God were, in fact, "just like the pictures," which were, of course, White. But God was visualized as White because the power in America was in White hands, rather than because of any massive and profound self-rejection among earlier slaves. These visions illustrated that Blacks were pragmatic enough to seek out power whether it be black, white, purple or polka dot. The crucial consideration was that this High God with all his power, even though not Black, did accept Blacks and did will their freedom. Slaves selectively seized and emphasized scriptural images like po' man Lazarus in Jesus' parable,[8] and events like the Exodus. It was a wise use of Scripture, even though Moses and God were at times confused in the minds of some slaves.

White Religious Exposure

This Moses/God confusion was not born of gross ignorance, even though this would have been understandable in the face of the barriers of new language with no teachers. Rather, it was born of a much concealed failure of many masters to permit an even minimal exposure to Christian ideas, or access to corporate worship. When the suggestion is made that master-sponsored Christianity became a straitjacket to harness Black yearnings for freedom,[9] it overlooks the smallness of the percentage of Blacks who were ever permitted an adequate White religious exposure, as over against the vitality of the underground church or cult. Even the "well-treated" slaves' autobiographies do not show much White effort to proselytize, and even less Black credulity. On the surface, Blacks related to White Christianity as "massa" expected, but they had their own ways of worship, as well as of dealing with the White religion which they so easily sensed to be false and manipulative.

A wide variety of religious arrangements prevailed across the South, as indicated. It is portrayed by the following quotations from the autobiographies, given in some detail because of their great importance in understanding how much independent and even secret Black religion there was during slavery, and why.

Scott beat her husband a lot of times because he caught him praying. But "beatings didn't stop my husband from praying. He just kept on. . . ." They didn't have any Bible on the Scott plantation she said, for it meant a beating or "a killing if you'd be caught with one. . . ." When the slaves went to church . . . sat in the rear . . . sermon was never preached to the slaves. [South Carolina][10]

My boss didn' 'low us to go to church, er to pray and sing. Iffen he ketched us prayin' or singin' he whupped us. . . . But he wa'nt mean to his niggers, 'cept for doin' things he don't 'low us to. [Virginia, Louisiana, Mississippi][11]

Well, my old marster . . . was a Methodist preacher. He didn't do us like he was a preacher, though. . . . No, mam, they wasn't allowed to have prayer meeting or nothing like a meeting. If a nigger got religion they said he was crazy. Sometimes I would go to church with the white folks, to see after the children, but the niggers wasn't allowed to go to church. . . . Some of the slaves got religion anyhow. [Tennessee][12]

Them circuit ridin' preachers come to the white church and tries to make the white folks bring their slaves to preaching. Preacher say, 'Nigger have a soul to save as us all.' Massa allus went to church but I don't 'lieve it done him any good, 'cause while he there at meetin' the niggers in the field stacking fodder. [Texas, born in Alabama][13]

We went to church on the place and you ought to have heared that preachin'. Obey your massa and missy, don't steal chickens and eggs, and meat, but nary a word 'bout havin' a soul to save. [Texas][14]

Didn't have no colored churches. De drivers and de overseers, de house-servants, de bricklayers and folks like dat'd go to de white folk's church. But not de field hands. Why dey couldn't have all got in de church. . . . But them as went would *sing!* Oh they'd sing! . . . They had colored preachers to preach to de field hands down in de quarters. . . . Meet next day to de marsa's and turn in de report. How many pray, how many ready for baptism and all like dat. Used to have Sabbath School in de white people's . . . porch, on Sunday evening . . . fill dat porch! . . . Learn . . . de Catechism. [South Carolina][15]

Sometimes, dey makes de slaves go to church. De white folks sot up fine in de carriage . . . den all de slaves walks front de carriage till dey gits to church. De slaves sot outside under de shade trees. If de preacher talk real loud, you can hear him out de window. [Texas/Louisiana][16]

Go to white people church and sit out of doors and wait till dey come out and den go in and have preaching. . . . White preacher. [South Carolina][17]

Us niggers used to have a prayin' ground down in the hollow and sometime we come out of the field, between 11 and 12 at night, scorchin' and burnin' up with nothing to eat, and we wants to ask the good Lawd to have mercy. . . . Some gits so joyous they starts to holler loud and we has to stop up they mouth. I see niggers git so full of the Lawd and so happy they draps unconscious. [Texas/? Very common][18]

We didn't have no place to go to church, but old Master didn't care if we had singing and praying, and we would tie our shoes on our backs and go down the road close to the white church and set down and put our shoes on and go up close and listen to the service. [Oklahoma/?][19]

It is, of course, not surprising that quite a few Blacks were not formal Christians and didn't plan to become so. African tradition had not had such regular public religious observances anyway, so "some [good folks] went to chu'ch and some went fishin' on Sunday." [Mississippi][20] Others went along with the system on the surface, but they were quite aware of injustice in worship. Alice Woodward recalled her wedding day, when she was married by the white preacher after morning service. "I 'members de song de white folks sung dat day. 'Hark from de tomb de doleful sound.' Don't you think that a wrong song to sing on de weddin' day? 'Joy to de world' was in our heart and dat tune would have been more 'propriate, seems to me." [South Carolina][21]

Polly Colbert also went along with the system, at least to the extent that she showed little rancor when reporting the monumental racism and pride of her frontier [Oklahoma/?] master and his fellows, who only had brush arbors themselves: "Father Murrow preached for de white folks . . . and us colored folks went to church wid dem. Dey had church under brush arbors and we set off to ourselves but we could take part in de singing and sometimes a colored person would get happy and shout but nobody didn't think nothing 'bout dat."[22]

However, no amount of surface permissiveness should be allowed to mask the utter contempt in which the vast majority of slaves held their masters' religion. And no volume of records of official permission to engage in limited worship should be allowed to cover the widespread denial of any thorough exposure to Christianity for slaves. We shall eventually return to the contempt, but consideration of access to white religion should not be concluded without a word or two about the more northern slave states not covered by the WPA narratives.

Escaped slave William Craft reported a legal indictment from the "advanced" Commonwealth of Virginia, County of Norfolk, charging that Margaret Douglass "moved and instigated by the devil, wickedly . . . and feloniously, on the fourth day of July, in the year of our Lord [1854] . . . did teach a certain black girl named Kate to read in the Bible, to the great displeasure of Almighty

God, to the pernicious example of others in like case offending, contrary to the form of the statute in such case provided, and against the peace and dignity of the Commonwealth of Virginia." The judge added his own comment that she was "guilty of one of the vilest crimes that ever disgraced society. . . . No enlightened society can exist where such offences go unpunished."[23] For this felony she was sentenced to a month in the county jail.

J. W. C. Pennington, another escaped slave, grew up under similar circumstances in the border state of Maryland. The resistance to the evangelization of slaves was so great that he had never heard of Jesus nor seen a whole Bible in his life, at the time of his escape.[24] In Maryland, the speaker at Black funerals (usually when the slaves had a day off, and long after burial) was a Black volunteer whose efforts to dignify the departures of his brethren was not able to include Scripture or doctrines for the comfort and instruction of the living. He was limited to hymns and singing, fervent prayers, and impressive, impromptu exhortations of his own design. A White Methodist preacher at a nearby camp meeting was placed on trial for his life for addressing words of comfort to the slaves.[25]

Other slaves in other areas reported the same limits on the mind and proclamations of Black preachers, some of whom would "read" from their hands, being unable to read and legally forbidden to own a Bible. Many slaves reported that they simply endured White preachers, but that it was "heaven" when they could hear a Black preacher. They were usually not implying that these ingenious Black men of God had been permitted an even minimal exposure to the breadth of the Christian faith. There is a report that when the crops were harvested the slaves were permitted to go fifteen miles away to a camp meeting. But this was indeed unusual, especially when escorted only by a trusted slave. The "mildest form of slavery" existed in Maryland; and if the religious restrictions Pennington suggests were true there, what must it have been like further South?

Black religion distinctly was not a gift of the White man, no matter what parts he may have supplied wittingly or no. Rather,

Black religion, in its pervasive form, was nothing less than an underground folk phenomenon, subversive of slavery, and supportive of Black survival. It used praise houses, brush arbors, and just hollow places and forest clearings, for its prayers, songs, ring shouts and fellowship, and it was later to be aptly labeled the "invisible institution" by E. Franklin Frazier.

Channels of White Contributions

Some channels of White contributions (as restricted as they were, contrary to popular myth) did exist among the religious arrangements just considered. Blacks found ways to gain access to the religious resources they needed. The Bible, for instance, came somehow to be fairly accurately understood and used as the oral tradition of Blackamerican religion, just as the proverbs in the previous chapter were the well-stated encapsulations of the African traditional religious wisdom. The clarity and relevance of the selected passages of the Bible offered, in fact, the favorite means of expressing Black creative and contemporary adaptation of their previous African world view. These passages still loom large in the Black tradition. No amount of massive secularization of American life is likely soon to separate the Black church masses from the summation of their African faith and wisdom which they appropriated from the King James translation of a comparable corpus of Hebrew folk faith.

These scriptural sayings surface in folk songs, both spiritual and "secular," in simple folk comments, as found in the slave narratives noted above, and in the folk preaching. Of the latter we have no records, save the folk memory of the narratives, and this is all from the later slave period (nineteenth century), as opposed to the earliest slave sermons. This forces us to reason back from earliest records, to develop a likely model of slave exposure to the Bible and of choosing favorites out of its vast varieties of wisdom.

In so reasoning back, we must assume the integrity of the slave and resist the widespread tendency to consider as valid only alien influences on the Black mentality. The evidence of slave sophistication and resources to maintain that integrity is abundant. Once this is granted, it becomes easy to see that Blacks acquired biblical sayings everywhere they could be found—from overheard conversations and worship, to teaching and conversation, to formal participation worship, to the wise instruction of an occasional literate slave or free Black. The process was based on a genius for responding to and quickly memorizing and relating to any appealing biblical gem within earshot. It also involved a perhaps unconscious but growing flow of Black-to-Black religious conversation which by its underground nature was able to increase from a trickle to a flood and this became an acknowledged religion and culture for a significant number of people. The African priests turned preacher were perhaps the leaders of this growth among the invisible people and their equally invisible cult; but the religious genius of the total group is manifest, even after the crushing increases in dehumanization that took place in the early nineteenth century, after the invention of the cotton gin. It is safe to say, however, that Black culture and with it "the faith, Baby," were well on their way to formation prior to the early years of the last century.

The criteria for the slaves' choice of religious folk themes grew out of spontaneous, existential reactions to biblical exposures, in the light of their own original culture and world view. They responded, first, to that which so obviously and easily matched their previous belief. This constituted a considerable volume. The famous Gustavus Vassa's early slave narrative illustrates this well, in describing the teaching given him aboard ship by a well-educated fellow crew member:

He taught me to shave and dress hair a little, and also to read the Bible, explaining many passages to me, which I did not comprehend. I was wonderfully surprised to see the laws and rules of my own country written almost exactly here; a circumstance which I believe tended to impress our [African] manners and customs more deeply on my memory. I used to tell him of this resemblance.[26]

A second subtle criterion was surely the appeal of the usefulness of Christian themes in the experience to which they were
subjected. It is with a strange and uncanny accuracy that they
seem to have zeroed in on useful material, having had so much
less than a comprehensive exposure to the Bible. They were not
brainwashed by the distortions and wrong emphases, but picked
up between the lines of White folks' bad exegesis not only the
original and beclouded text, but its relevance for their condition.

A third criterion may have been the simple response to the
appeal of a new idea. The African would likely have responded
spontaneously and communicated speedily. We must remember,
again, that it was his non-Western habit to give a hearing to *all*
views and to take on the religions of conquered as well as con-
queror, fusing the best of each. He was not beset with a desire to
have and to hold the only "authentic" version of anything.

An interesting model of the interaction between the two main
religious traditions is unintentionally spelled out in the slave
narrative of Sabe Rutledge of Waccamaw, Georgetown County,
South Carolina:

Sunday come go to church in that same blue shirt! Little old pole church
[brush arbor]—(gone now)—call "Dick Green Bay Church." (Named for
a local character.) When we go to church before freedom, Mudder and
them have to have the ticket [slave pass]. . . . Old man Zachariah Duncan
been the preacher. That the same man build the first "Heaven Gate"
[Baptist] church after freedom. He got drift lumber on the river and on
the beach. Flat 'em—make a raft and float 'em over to the hill and the
men haul 'em to "Heaven Gate" with ox. Yes, "Heaven Gate" built outer
pick up lumber. [Milled lumber lost in a shipwreck.] . . . Before freedom
Parson Glennie—he was [E]piscopal—he would come give us a service
once a month on the plantation.[27]

This is the same Alexander Glennie whose *Sermons Preached
on Plantations to Congregations of Negroes* was published in
1844.[28] Rector of All-Saints Parish, Waccamaw, he was noted as
a "liberal" of the Southern sort, as evidenced by his sermons. I
is probable that he was as "dangerous" a writer as would be

permitted to stay in print—or even among the living, if the death of David Walker is any measure. Walker was mysteriously killed in Boston for writing against the institution of slavery. Glennie's book was acceptable although it contained only one sermon on the subject of willing servitude. Its text was Ephesians 6:7: "With good will doing service, as to the Lord, and not to men." There were twenty-five others which came no closer than the one from Acts 5:2, against lying. He said much about repentance for sin, and made the mistake of telling the story of the Last Judgment in Matthew 25:31. Thus he no doubt leaked the true Christian view of who is accounted saved—on what humane grounds God's judgment is rendered. In fact, much of Glennie's material on heaven and the resurrection and who is the greatest in the kingdom of God was vulnerable to relevant appropriation by freedom-seeking Blacks.

So the Heaven Gate members had service under the master on the plantation, with a very dull Episcopal presentation by Glennie. And they had a brush-arbor Black worship, which later became the Heaven Gate Church. Out of the revivalistic themes of the former they no doubt obtained the new idea of a place called hell. And they dealt with it so seriously (here and everywhere) that hell became a ruling consideration in motivating conversion to Christianity of the formal sort. Thus the "liberal" tendency of Glennie, to preach to Blacks the very same moralisms and motives that he preached to Whites, not only heightened Blacks' awareness of their possession of equally human souls; it caused them to be concerned to avert their loss in hell. But the most important non-African acquisition here was hell as a place for the *masters* to go.

This last factor is more than probably the major reason for the strength of so new a concept as hell fire and damnation. Thus what appears at first sight to be a racial catastrophe, generating new Black guilt feelings, may have started out as a positive reading of a handy place for God to mete out proper justice to cruel masters. Whatever severity God may have had for errant Blacks, he had a manifold greater portion for their oppressors. Slaves

literally *enjoyed* and *celebrated* their certainty that ol' massa
was already in flames. The transition from an African concept
of corporate guilt to a more Western individual guilt and hell
punishment yielded at least that much of positive value.

Attributes of God

We have examined at some length the importance of High God
in Yoruba and other West African religions. The idea of God now
must be viewed as Blackamericans adapted it in the ways just
mentioned, of useful incorporations from Christianity, as they
perceived that faith. The most obvious change was at the point
of the ineffability or transcendence of God. A Black Pentecostal
scholar, Leonard Lovett, suggests that in the Pentecostal experience the Holy Spirit's supernatural gifts underscore transcendence, while the personal nature of the experience amounts to a
self-manifestation of the deity in the life of the person. Thus is
fused into one experience both the immanence and transcendence of God.[29]

While Lovett speaks of one denominational tradition, he might
well have spoken for all of early Black folk religion, if one does
not rigidly insist on glossolalia as a part of the experience. Africans had long had a tradition of possession by lesser deities, and
the expressive and emotionally cathartic experience continued
on these shores. When Blacks heard that, according to the good
news of the New Testament, God was in Christ and that he was
also in men generally, or could be, they evolved an understanding that the beings which had possessed them were in fact only
one, and that this One was none other than the third person of
the Trinity, the Holy Spirit or Holy Ghost. This affirmation and
adaptation of African roots was not without European parallels
in the shouting of Methodists in Wales and on the Western frontier of America, but it was a fuller expression, with a much
longer history of continuous practice. Its permanence is obvious
and its blessing and enrichment to the Christian tradition is

likewise evident. Blacks thus developed a means of participation in Christian worship which involved the whole human body, affirming and expressing it, rather than denying and repressing it. It is probable that this African, holistic praise of God was also such an important affirmation of Black selfhood that its sense of "God all in me" was among the most important resources for survival in the unprecedented dehumanization of American slavery. We shall look at this again in the section on the Holy Spirit.

There were other aspects or attributes of God which were to remain relatively unchanged, except for the language in which they were expressed. One of these, related to immanence, is the omnipresence of God. One-hundred-five-year-old Henry Necaise of Mississippi summed it up when he, having adjusted his church affiliations to what was available, declared, "I figgers dat God is ever'where."[30] Close to this was the folk doctrine of omniscience, a belief expressed both in Christianity and in the praise-names of God in West Africa, indicating that God sees "all you do and hears all you say." Slave masters were to make unjust use of this doctrine, but they would never have been able to use it so well had it not been there already.

The omnipotence of God was likewise well established in Black folk belief, as we have seen in the last chapter. And rather than a literal fatalism, as has been indicated, it was a means of affirming that the whole world was in the hands of one powerful enough to handle it. The timing of the exercise of that power was not always to the liking of the Black man, but the existence of that power was his only hope. He was not about to posit a more chaotic and less unified principle of being and source of power.

As we have seen, this omnipotence logically led to a strong theory of predestination. While making man quite responsible for his acts regarding the manageable aspects of his destiny, it confidently left to God the things beyond man's all-too-obvious limits. This was affirmation of life at its best, and eventually it was justified by the very destruction (legally, on paper) of that most hated of institutions, slavery. Sallie Paul said, *"God* set de slaves free. De Lord do it. It just like dis, I believes it was intended from God for de slaves to be free en Abraham Lincoln was just de one what present de speech. It was revealed to him en God was de one dat stepped in en fight de battle." [South Carolina][31]

Others fully believed that Lincoln was as raised up by God as was Moses. They knew that "what God got 'lot out for a man he'll get it."[32] And if they were inclined to question, they did not do so for long. James Weldon Johnson captured their folk belief when he placed in the mouth of the Black preacher the words, "Young man—Young man—Your arm's too short to box with God."[33] Fortunately that God was a gracious being, and his will was for the good of mankind. Ed Barber quite casually mentioned that he returned to the old Barber place "and marry de gal de Lord always 'tended for me to marry."[34] Predestination, in this case, could have been bypassed, but the witness evidenced an utterly practical and everyday understanding that the powerful God was wise enough and concerned enough to give him a good wife.

This affirmation of life, implicit in previous folk doctrines, was explicit in God as Creator. The Ashanti hawk flew over and said that all the Creator made was beautiful, which was a way of saying that God was good because his creation was evidence, and it was good. The idea of what God made and why he made it ran through ordinary conversation, with or without Christian exposure. The idea that he had made it good was taken for granted by the slaves, and it produced a positive attitude, assuming the long-range good of *all* experience. It also affirmed the goodness of the things of earth which God created for here and now, and caused Blacks unashamedly to strive for them as both spiritual and material goals which could not be separated. This was true of freedom, but it was true of all else. The idea that slaves sang "You can have all this world, give me Jesus," indicating excessive otherworldliness, is erroneous. There was not and is not a more earthy religious tradition in America than that of the Blacks, and this earthiness stems from a deep, visceral certainty about a spiritual source of all being, a Creator who is still in charge, with *none* of his work worthy of being called common or unclean.

Justice and Righteousness of God

The Black believer moves on to the idea of God as also just and righteous. The affirmation of life and the indispensability of its certain meaningfulness—the beneficence of Creator and the benevolence of creation—were and are necessarily supported by the certainty of the justice of God. But it must be understood that when Blacks faced the gross evils of slavery, they laid much more claim to God's justice than to his grace. For this reason this topic of justice will be more lengthily treated than any other attribute of God.

J. Deotis Roberts has expressed Black folk faith in the following introduction to justice: "All-power is a precious attribute of God for black people; for them impotent goodness has little appeal . . . a God who is absolute in both power and goodness makes sense to black men. . . . Absolute power ensures the ultimate triumph of the good; but absolute goodness assures us that absolute power will not be abused."[35]

All else depended on this combination of omnipotence and ethics. In fact, the eloquent and frequent expressions of the glory of God, another praise attribute, were subtle statements of God's justice and power. The glory-of-God theme implied the smallness and insignificance of the master's finery and power, and thus was a form of protest in disguise. The words of the spiritual were a similarly coded assertion of the justice and omnipotence of God. "My God is so high, you can't git over him; he's so low, you can't git under him; he's so wide, you can't git around him; you must come in by and through the Lamb." If questions arise as to what this meant, remember that there was never more than potty agreement with the massive attempts to prove to slaves that God had willed their servitude. *No* spiritual ever hinted at anything but God's disapproval of the "peculiar institution."

For many it seems strange indeed that a people so deprived and depressed could know so well and believe so deeply in the justice of God. If one assumes, with me, the impressive sensitivity and

integrity of the slaves, one surely knows that they were not gullible enough to accept the teaching of God's justice by a slave
master with a whip in his hand. Nor would a master have
breathed such a doctrine in more than an obviously slanted and
propagandistic way, dealing only with slaves and not with himself. The source of this wondrous faith and wisdom is, of course,
their African faith and world view.

Once a slave believed deeply in God's justice, he could detect
signs of its operation in many places and ways. Mrs. Nancy Howard, an escapee from Maryland living in Ontario, reported that

one Sunday my master promised me and my boy, that he hoped God
would damn him, if he did not tie us up and whip us the next morning.
I went into a corner and prayed to God, to allow me to take all the
whipping, but to spare my boy. By and by, my mistress ran for me; she
said 'your master is dying!' I blew the horn to call people to us. . . . He
seemed to have his senses—he would make signs with his head. He would
allow no one to pray with him. I prayed for him all the time he was sick.
[He lived a week.][36]

Mrs. Howard was free to pray for him simply because she was
so sure of God's justice. Her faith is indicative of a moral superiority and spiritual genius of which she was not aware. There
were many others who could see easily the terrible degradation
to which slave masters and their families were reduced, in the
process of the justice of God.

The heart of Sojourner Truth bled for her owners after one of
the family had murdered his wife in cold blood, but it did not
bleed enough to prevent her from seeing in it a "special providence of God. She thought she saw clearly, that their unnatural
bereavement was a blow dealt in retributive justice: but she
found it not in her heart to rejoice over them."[37] This is especially
noble in the light of the fact that the murdered woman's mother
had laughed at Sojourner Truth's deep concern for her own son,
and the fact that the murderer himself had beaten her son so
badly that she had prayed, "Oh Lord, 'render unto them double'
for all this!"[38]

Slave narratives reveal deep sensitivity to the fact that slave ownership brutalized and degraded the character of the owner. Frederick Douglass's new mistress in Baltimore is another good case in point. "The fatal poison of irresponsible power, and the natural influence of slavery customs, were not long in making a suitable impression on the gentle and loving disposition of my excellent mistress. . . . It took several years to change the sweetness of her temper into fretful bitterness."[39]

A more wholesale description of the process of justice, as seen in the deterioration of masters, is apparent in this excerpt from J. W. C. Pennington's *Fugitive Blacksmith:*

As far back as I can recollect, indeed, it was a remark among slaves, that every generation of slaveholders are more and more inferior. There were several large and powerful families in our country, including that of my master, which affords to my mind a melancholy illustration of this remark. . . . General R., a brother-in-law to my master, owned a large and highly valuable tract of land . . . slaves . . . the number was large . . . a splendid mansion. . . . He was a member of Congress. . . . He had numerous . . . children. . . . General R. himself ran through his vast estate, died intemperate, and left a widow and large number of daughters, some minors, destitute, and none of his sons fitted for any employment but in the army and navy.[40]

It is not difficult to understand why "sowing and reaping," a theme already well known in African world view, was popular in Black folk religion. One ex-slave said in his advanced years: "I am . . . never sick. I live close to the Lord. He will not forsake them that walk upright. In Genesis 6 and 7 it says, 'Be not deceived, God is not mocked, whatsoever a man soweth, that shall he also reap.'"[41] The fact that it was Galatians and not Genesis is immaterial. He knew the chapter and verse and, most of all, the meaning for Black survival. Two verses after the above quotation was another Black favorite: "And let us not grow weary in well-doing, for in due season we shall reap, if we faint not."[42]

Slaves delighted in phrases like "due season" and "by and by"; indeed such phrases have not yet lost their appeal. Another popular "Bible" verse was, "The race is not to the swift, nor the battle to the strong, but to him that holds out to the end." The fact that this saying combined elements from Ecclesiastes and Matthew did not matter. It was a part of the folk Bible, and its truth was and is indisputable. It is also a perfect example of appropriations that matched the original African world view.

In addition to the religious genius and sensitivity that was manifested by slaves, it must be conceded that some of their sound understandings came to them from sincere White Christians. Many instances of Quakers and Methodists teaching biblical truth "like it is" occurred after slaves had escaped. But there were instances of bold truth expressed in the heart of slave country. These, too, added to the Black understanding of the justice of God. Allen Manning, an Oklahoman born in Mississippi, reported the brutal beating of an escaped and captured slave, by his master, a Baptist preacher. A White deacon stopped it thus: "Old Deacon Sears stand it as long as he can and then he step up and grab old Master's arm and say, 'Time to stop, Brother! I'm speaking in the name of Jesus!' Old Master quit then, but he still powerful mad."[43]

The justice of God was certain. The problem was simply a matter of knowing *when* it would be applied. A Yoruba proverb mentioned in the last chapter was a prayer asking to live long enough to see the evil oppressor punished, but it was phrased as a petition for the evil to live long enough to "get his" in plain sight of the oppressed. The slave view was not quite so certain of this-worldly punishment, but it did match exactly the African view, so very common, that evil must surely come to an end. They sang, "I'm so glad, trouble don't last always. Oh my Lord . . ." It could mean that "death come creepin' in my room" to terminate my trouble, or it could mean that God was going at last to act. Victoria Perry's mother in South Carolina told her, "Some day we are going to be free; the Good Lord won't let this go on all the time."[44] Her mother lived long enough to see the fruits of her faith and shouted when the general told them they were free.

The realistic facing of the fact that "you can't hold a watch [time piece] on God" is far from an escapist or fatalistic statement. It is a reaffirmation of the conviction that God is just, and that the realities of human existence are positive. Life *is* worth living.

"Due season" could be, as a matter of last resort, the very Judgment Day itself. If God didn't punish master here on earth, there was at least the dead certainty that he would mete out justice at the final Judgment. Sister Kelly, probably of Tennessee, stated it with easy flow. "Jest remember that you got to stand before the most holy of all, God a'mighty, every deed you done, you gotta give strict account of. . . . Don't never forgit that."[45] Slaves sang that "sinners will be running in that Great Day," and asked, with Master no doubt in mind, "Who shall be able to stand?"

Of course, even Sister Kelly was not always completely sure. When her husband died, she was frank to confess, she was prone to question for a time. " 'Lord, . . . why did you take him away from me?' Poor me, I said, 'Lord you took him away from me.' Well, he spoke to me agin, and he said, 'I will forever open the way and provide for you,' . . . and he sho' has done it, too, I tell you."[46] Many slaves experienced these very human responses, but their return to an affirmation of faith expressed not an easy or escapist answer, but a kind of determination to hang on to a reason for living.

The slaves not only lived this faith, but far more than is widely written of, kept up a running opposition to the slave system. It was their solid conviction that God was not the least in favor of slavery. William Craft voted his conviction with his feet when he escaped. He stated it: "There is, however, great consolation in knowing that God is just, and will not let the oppressor of the weak, and the spoiler of the virtuous, escape unpunished here and hereafter."[47] He was the famous man whose wife of light hue disguised herself as his male master and escaped all the way from Georgia with him.

The convicted henchmen of Nat Turner's Rebellion were known to have "declared that they was going [dying] happy fore that God had a hand in what they was doing."[48]

Pennington had a theological statement which needs to be in this record, but the gut-level world view of slaves was never so precisely phrased while it was so eloquently lived by. "He has permitted us to be enslaved according to the invention of wicked men, instigated by the devil, with intention to bring good out of the evil, but He does not, He cannot approve of it. He has no need to approve of it, even on account of the good which He will bring out of it, for He could have brought about that very good in some other way."[49]

John Martin of Ontario stated it more typically when he said, "Slavery is a dreadful thing. Slaveholders—I know not what will become of them. Some of them I love—but I know they deserve punishment, and leave them in the hands of God."[50] Many others were not so kind and noncommittal as to what would happen in the hands of God. Mrs. Sutton of Tennessee complained about the hard work she had to do, as a woman: "You would have to do everything, and some of them very same devils what made you do it are in hell burning now."[51]

Rev. Charlie Moses of Mississippi was likewise specific. "My master was mean and cruel. . . . The God Almighty has condemned him to eternal fiah. Of that I is *certain.*"[52] One-hundred-year-old Mary Reynolds of Texas raised her certainty to the level of celebration when she reported outright joy in contemplating her slave driver's eternal fate.

We was scart of Solomon and his whip, though, and he didn't like frolickin'. He didn't like for us niggers to pray, either. We never heard of no church, but us have prayin' in the cabins. We'd set on the floor and pray with our heads down low and sing low, but if Solomon heared he'd come and beat on the wall with the stock of his whip. He'd say, "I'll come in there and tear the hides off you backs." But some the old niggers tell us we got to pray to Gawd that he don't think different of the blacks and the whites. I know that Solomon is burnin' in hell today, and it *pleasures* me to know it.[53]

Slaves were equally certain about where the hand of God would deposit them, as well as the nitty gritty limits of earthly joys: "Does I believe in 'ligion? What else good for colored folks? I ask you if dere ain't a heaven, what's colored folks got to look forward to? They can't get anywhere down here. De only joy they can have here, is servin' and lovin'; us can git dat in 'ligion, but dere is a limit to de nigger in everything else."[54]

In summary, then, the slave narratives indicate a simple but resilient and serviceable certainty that life could not possibly be as evil, ultimately, as it then appeared to be. The Creator who showed his justice in the accurately diagnosed deterioration of masters and their whole families—that same God would show his justice in the ultimate destiny of each oppressed slave, on one or the other side of chilly Jordan. While God's justice took into account "how you talk" and "what you talkin' about," the spiritual warning that "you better mind" (because "you got to give account at the Judgment morning") was likely more concerned with careless slave talk bringing the loose-lipped servant to a master's kangaroo judgment. The full-fledged judgment slaves believed in was reserved for the master himself, and that prospect was a cause for literal celebration.

There have, however, always been some who dissented from the majority Black view of the justice of God. William R. Jones of Yale Divinity School maintains that most Black theologians writing currently cannot celebrate God's justice until they have established it. This is a part of the "theodicy" which he contends has to be the first order of business for any theology styled as a theology of liberation. He is saying that Black theologians may not even need to develop a "theology" or "word about God" if, as might be the case inside their system, they could wind up finding that God is in fact not just, according to liberation standards.[55]

Persons who might style themselves as adherents to the "orthodoxy" (a terribly un-African term) of Black folk belief, which never pretended to be "theological" in the intellectual sense, must nevertheless face the challenges Jones raises. One may not lightly dismiss the intellectual cream of Black womanhood and manhood, or ask them to cease all rational thought about God. If there is no Black way to "love the Lord with all thy mind," in

1975, one could make a pragmatic case for Black adaptability which would forsake "irrational" religion of the past in order to survive in a complex technological age.

Also, since Black faith and thought are as various as any of those of other ethnic traditions, the differences between schools of thought are not settled by means of argument about who is the blackest. The folk majority's beliefs can merit continued adherence only if they can satisfactorily meet the same challenges raised in Jones's internal criticism of the theology of liberation. Thus Black certainties about the justice of God are confronted with Jones's concerns with the status of suffering. Can unmerited and therefore unjust suffering be eliminated? What is its cause? If there be a variety of possible causes, how does one determine the cause in a given instance? Is it a mystery involving punishment from God and beyond understanding? Is God a White racist in permitting massive, transgenerational suffering to Blacks in a type and intensity incapable of any traditional interpretation as redemptive?

Jones warns against any faith which, knowingly or unwittingly, evolves into a conceptual prop for oppression. He also wants to be sure that any peace of mind born of faith is not in fact a form of quietism that declines responsibility for unremitting attempts at change, including rebellion if need be.

It is my strong conviction that the best of Black folk belief has historically answered all of these challenges and well. It has never assumed that God willed negative suffering or oppression. The corpus of the spirituals and the illustrations above are in point. The believing majority has always assumed that *something* could and should be done to reduce and ultimately to eliminate such evils as slavery. When the universal presence of violent "paterollers" and predictably unfair White witnesses (Blacks couldn't be heard in court) made the deep South a kind of deep dungeon from which there was no possible escape, the slaves turned to massive prayer as an alternative to doing absolutely nothing. The pervasive belief in the power of these petitions to God, among Black *and* White, is evident in the fact that they were so strictly forbidden by "Christian" masters.

Slaves of faith did more than pray, even in the deep South. They attacked the system on every hand. They "stole" the food they had earned and needed, requiring phony White religion to spend ludicrous lengths of sermon time inveighing against stealing massa's pigs and chickens. Some of the most prayerful were in on the appropriation of food, as well as the affectation of jovial laziness or chronic health problems. There was also a *loyal refusal of small children* (deeply indoctrinated in resistance) *to reveal vital information,* no matter how much they wanted the candy bribe. They learned how to give misinformation and "keep the faith," while gaining the candy. "They used to tell me if I would tell them what they wanted to know that they would give me some candy. . . . I liked candy very much, but never could hardly get it. They would give me the candy but I would only tell them they went away, and I didn't know where they went, just went away."[56]

One ex-slave, born in Eden, Tennessee, in 1844, told how children got this way. Her mother's saintly faith was illustrated when she called master and slaves alike to her deathbed and declared, "I'm going where there ain't no fighting and cussing and damning." But her faith commanded her to teach her daughter to fight. She told her small daughter never to let anyone abuse her. "I'll kill you, gal, if you don't stand up for yourself. Fight, and if you can't fight, kick; if you can't kick, then bite." Her mother practiced what she preached, and she nearly killed her mistress for trying to whip her. Then she violently and successfully avoided being punished by two armed professional nigger beaters.[57]

The most obvious form of religious resistance was in the preaching act itself. Solomon Oliver of Oklahoma, formerly of Mississippi, told of his father: "Father use to preach to the slaves when a crowd of them could slip off into the woods. I don't remember much about the religious things, only just what Daddy told me when I was older. He was caught several times slipping off to the woods and because he was a preacher I guess they layed on the lash a little harder trying to make him give up preaching."[58]

Many accounts of refusal to stop preaching are available, and some preachers were beaten, had their backs pickled with salt, and eventually died for their resistance. Black folk religion's track record in forbidden preaching is answer enough to the challenge of quietism. "They done all they knew to do." And their descendants launched the current revolution in Black rights and dignity from a religious or church base.

As for God's theoretical potential for racism, as raised by William Jones,[59] the evidence has already been made clear. Blacks *knew* God was not pleased with slavery. They looked forward to and back at the Emancipation in the same way that the Jews viewed the Exodus. Moderns may need more of a rationale, but this is not difficult. To be truly made in God's image and capable of choice, *man must be free.* Therefore, for a season, God is permissive even allowing for slavery and massive White racism. Black folk theology easily and gladly answers all of the stock questions. It only withdraws when Black intellectual theology insists that to be believed God's justice and benevolence must be demonstrated on our terms. What more can be said than has already been said, except that the concrete readings of God's justice by slaves might never have occurred if the slave had not already believed in a just God. For those so singly focused on liberation more "proof" may be necessary, but "demonstration" is not possible. And neither is it possible to demonstrate a denial or disproof of the justice of God.

Black folk theology, despite its record of highly liberating activity, cannot properly be labeled exclusively a theology of liberation. Black masses unanimously intuit such a goal, but do not self-consciously characterize their beliefs as a body primarily designed for liberation. It is more likely a theology of existence or survival, whose affirmation of selfhood logically denies all hindrances to full being, including slavery and oppression. Black masses have long looked on the deterioration of the masters and the curses visited on the oppressors, and they have found no desire to be White. They have proudly seen for centuries their moral and spiritual superiority to the oppressor. They have not pitied themselves, nor considered their lack of liberty an ultimate curse.

Thus the Black saints through the centuries would lay no claim to a unique brand of suffering of proportions that would threaten the very justice of God. Sophisticated Blacks would know that Black suffering's transgenerational record will never match that of the lowest caste in India. Medieval historians indicate that wives and daughters of serfs were fair sex game for feudal lords. As horrible as slavery was, many Black women had more protection than many serfs. Thus the slavery experience and the present wilderness travail are, for the Black folk believer, neither unique nor traumatically inexplicable.

The answer to the possibility that God may have forsaken Blacks is given in the very first Black folk assumptions about God, which are also assumptions about life. They are the two sides of the same coin, and no Black would ever dream of asking why all of life has gone sour. He would feel that it should be obvious that life is and always has been worth living. Existence has never been overwhelmingly negative. So Black folk tradition acts out its deepest grief at the funeral and then goes to the feast. It is not impossible that there is a fundamental harmony between this affirmation of life and the "functional ultimacy of man" which Professor Jones proposes as a prescriptive principle and alternative to the Black folk majority's theism.[60]

If life is good by a definition essential to its very living, *then God is righteous and just* by a similar definition. It may seem to be born of a reading of experience, but it logically precedes the reading and transcends it as well. The definition of God, if he *be* God, as just, is clearly a matter of Black faith through the centuries. God could not be described as capricious fate, capable of lowering injustices, and still elicit his title of God, no matter how powerful. This argument is and always has been more than a means of foreshortening debate and stifling questions. It is the other side of a sophisticated and human-welfare-serving appraisal of man's place in the universe. Despite all of our techno-logical "progress," that place in the universe has not changed very much. Mankind is still "tossed and driven on the restless sea of time" in the areas that matter most to his human existence. All men must face their limits, even while they are called to the enlargement of the boundaries of human knowledge and power at every point where the needs of mankind may be served. Inside those limits one either bets his life that God is just and the effort is worth it, or he does not, and is caught in a suicidal syllogism.

The assumption of God's justice is utterly beyond any "neutral" scrutiny or review, and is known and felt in God's possessing spiritual presence, in the same manner that God's existence and love are made mystically and existentially real. Questions are sometimes raised by the most trusting Black folk believers; but no matter how trying the crisis, the ultimate strength that stems from affirmation or belief is to be preferred over the threat to life of a world view of chaos.

It has been demonstrated that this belief was not overly in-dividualistic and quietistic, subjective, or counterrevolutionary. Serious risks were taken on the basis of this faith in resistance against slavery. Stereotypes of Black religious docility are ex-posed for what they really are when speaking of going "home to my Lord" is preceded in the spiritual by "Before I'd be a slave I'd be buried in my grave." If a man cannot see justice or strike meaningful blows in its behalf, he still need not despair, since his time frame gives God a longer span in which to "do his thing." Thus, present human need is served by a nonlinear time view which preserves the crucial option of faith.

Perhaps the most telling existential and pragmatic evidence for the Black belief system about the justice and righteousness of God is found in crises such as death, which bears on all other risks, options, and efforts. Blacks have traditionally accepted death in a healthy way, but this was inextricably bound up in trust in him who makes all men less than everlasting in this world. He even permits (not wills) that many persons come to untimely ends. At a recent California funeral, a Black Pentecostal layman, father of two nationally known professional athletes, said, "He's [God is] too wise to make a mistake and too just to be unfair." For him it was as natural as breathing to say such. In his life, all else proceeds from this assumption of faith. No man can "prove" that he and millions of Blacks like him are "wrong." Starting in prehistoric Africa, Blacks have walked with God long enough to develop this superior and very functional assumption regarding God and, inseparably, about life. There is no way to upset their theological "system" with arguments based on alien and *equally* a priori or unprovable foundations. In this sense, Black folk belief is coherently prepared to meet all challenges.

At any point in life, including death, the traditional Black can sing, with Black Methodist preacher Tindley, who wrote:

Trials dark on ev'ry hand, and we cannot understand
All the ways that God would lead us to that Blessed Promised Land;
But He guides us with His eye and we'll follow till we die,
For we'll understand it better by and by.[61]

As a Black Christian whose visceral responses are still in the pattern of the Black believer of the masses, I can intellectually and pragmatically suggest that the insights of this "other-worldly" hymn work very well to support life in this "low ground of sorrow." I literally sang and laid claim to these insights at the funeral of our twenty-six year old son (the fourth H. H. Mitchell), and I found it possible to feel and know that I was still capable of enjoying life. The delayed understanding of the ultimate processes of life is an existential aspect of the alternative to the denial of the justice and righteousness of God. Black existence has triumphed over the most absurd and unjust of experiences with this unshakable affirmation. Any gains I may have made over my foreparents, in powers (economic, political, or intellectual) in my generation have been offset by my gains in awareness of the injustices and in my sensitivity to them. Thus I feel the need of the faith of the Black Fathers all the more and not less.

This would include a traditionally Black and gut-level lifelong certainty that however you describe it, there is *some* kind of

awful and eternal fate reserved for inhumanity to the defense-
less, especially on the grand and premeditated scale suffered by
Blacks. Call it nonbeing, separation from God, or whatever, there
is an applicable correlate to the burning torment foreseen by
slaves for masters. If this is not so, then the White backlash
might as well surface and destroy America's Blacks and get it
over with. From the president of the country to the masses of
hard-hat laborers, or the members of the so-called silent
majority, there is no need to be careful if there is no divine
retribution. If stereotypical liberal thought is correct, and there
is no approximation of hell in the eternal schema, Blacks are
indeed in for hard going. Their violent efforts here will never
suffice to turn the tide of hysterical White racist guilt and com-
pensatory inhumanity, nor create enough hell in *this* life to serve
as a deterrent to racial injustice. Hell is still a part of the Black
man's *hope*.

In the ludicrous power game that permits the U.S.A. to
squander billions of dollars (to say nothing of lives) in South
Vietnam, and subsidize millionaire farmers and industrialists,
while retrenching in all humanitarian objectives, Black folk believers would find it hard to hold on if they didn't know who holds
the ultimate power and how He will ultimately use it. This existence is not unbearable, to be sure, and there is no desire whatever to trade places with the oppressor. But it "pleasures" Blacks
to the point of shouting and celebration just to know that God is
not mocked. This means that those who are at the bottom are not
mocked either, and whatever the oppressor sows he will surely
reap.

FIVE

American
Black Folk Beliefs

While Afro-American (and before it, African) religion had no systematic theology as such, its world view held together, supported by a network or "system" of strong component beliefs. For instance, undergirding the slaves' sweeping and unshakable faith in the justice and righteousness of God was a deeply ingrained positive view of reality. It explicitly included the *goodness of God,* the *goodness of all creation,* and the *goodness of life itself.* We have already seen this good creation reflected in the Ashanti proverb which quotes the hawk as viewing the earth from the air and saying, "All things the Supreme Being made are beautiful [good]."[1] The goodness of God was experienced in more intimate ways, however, than creation. The meaning of human experience was spelled out in powerful Christian affirmations of the grace and providence of God.

Slave belief combined the new and the old. Divine grace was, in a sense, a *new* understanding, growing out of newly acquired Christian views of individual sin. The Black acceptance of grace illustrated how a positive reading of life could be creatively supported in the face of newly discovered "sin" by means of selecting the compensating aspect of Christian belief. On the other hand, the positive view continued the traditional African belief in the doctrine of providence. This has been seen in the collec-

tion of West African proverbs on providence, one of which says
that God is the one who fans the flies for the cow who has no tail.[2]
The fact that slaves early and quite selectively acquired a view
of a grace not emphasized if even mentioned to them, while
tenaciously maintaining their belief in providence, is surely not
attributable to missionary teaching or other activity. Significant
White teaching, as we have seen, did not exist in the early years
of the formation of Black religious belief. Further, grand ideas
like these are not accepted, as it were, from alien instructors with
whips in their hands. Rather, this is monumental evidence of a
profound cultural bias and tenacity—a deeply ingrained positive
West African world view—operative at both conscious and unconscious levels.

Grace of God

There is impressive evidence that slaves overheard and were
influenced by ideas of the grace of God as early as by ideas of
individual sin and of hell. This was true despite the fact that the
faith among Whites did not give grace anything like "equal
time." It might be better to state that Blacks expropriated and
emphasized grace at the same time that they embraced the hell
which was demanded by divine justice in the face of the evils of
slavery. Thus they accepted a peril and with it a remedy, in an
intuitively balanced and realistic approach to grace. The content
assigned to grace is illustrated in the following excerpts from a
slave's conversion experience:

You see, I found the Lord all by myself;... When I 'fessed 'ligion, I didn't
see nothin; I just felt that I was free. Your spirit won't stay happy all the
time; but when you begins to feel downcas', you go back and seek the Lord
again. . . . The Lord reasoned unto me, and called me by my name, and
he said "I don't care what you once done; it's done [over with] for all the
time"; yes'm, that's what he said in a voice to me. He spoke to me so
sweet.[3]

Lest it be assumed that this forgiveness opened the door for the "cheap grace" to which theologians like Bonhoeffer have called attention, it is interesting to note how grace was applied to the eternal salvation of slavemasters.

I used to sit and listen, and I would sit night and day and hear the white folks plan mean things for the niggers. Sometimes I just can't see—God is a forgiving God, but sometimes I don't think he has forgiven the white people for the way they treated the poor black folks. . . .

I never saw a wedding until I was a great big gal. . . . All he [a slave] had to do was to ask old Master for the gal, and then if he said "Yes" all they had to do was to go on down and go to bed. One old Mistiss by the name of Fletcher would sometimes go and make them get up and tell them that married life was too good for them; and tell them to get up and get out and go to work. I know God didn't like that, and if he forgives the white folks for that, then I don't know what to think. . . .

But I ain't never seen how God can forgive those mean white folks for what they done to niggers way back yonder, nor for what they are doing to them now.[4]

The classic summary of the matter is expressed in the spiritual "I Gotta Shoe," which clearly refers to masters as hell-bound. "Ev'rybody talkin' 'bout heb'n ain't goin' there." Yet the slaves singing the song planned personally to "shout *all over* God's heb'n."

Thus did Blacks adapt and interpret grace from the raw materials available—from their own African bias or positive world view, from the bits and snatches of Christianity which they were able to scrounge, and from their own fusion of these two in practical and mystical experience. The slaves' understanding of grace met their existential needs, such as the need for identity ("The Lord . . . called me by my name") and the need for a sense of liberation ("I just felt that I was free"), and yet grace concepts included a sound and deep awareness of human frailty, Black and White. Black understandings of sin went far beyond the stereotypically petty moralities emphasized in the piety which prevailed among the unlearned and simplistic White exiles to America. Sin for Blacks undoubtedly included, also, the typical frontier revival negatives.

The taint of a petty piety full of "don'ts" and alien to African cultural expressions is seen in the attitude which prevailed among most slave believers concerning dancing. Almost every one of the hundreds of conversion stories available shows a conviction that dancing was worldly and sinful, and had to be given up before one could unite with the church. The testimony of an ex-slave in Mississippi is suggestive of the verbal if not visceral limits placed on grace: "When de time comes to go I hopes to be ready. De Lawd God Almighty takes good care o' his chillun [only] if dey be's good and holy [refrain from sins like dancing]."[5]

Such constricted grace probably reflects the narrower focus and increased rigidity resulting from the heightened oppression of Blacks in the 1890s and 1900s, but it was and is not restricted to that period. In my own ministry I have had to try to reclaim members excluded from the church in the 1920s for the simple act of social dancing. In fact, narrow grace is alive and well in many churches of limited insight and halfhearted strictness even today.

Nevertheless, the ingenious intuition of the more profound understanding of grace has always manifested itself frequently and eloquently. Charles Lyell's report of Andrew Marshall's early nineteenth-century sermon is illustrative. One can easily guess that there was a general emphasis on the petty moralities in Savannah, headquarters of the great revivalist George Whitefield; but no mention of minor moralities appears in the account. It does include a graphic description of an eagle swooping down to save the faltering eaglet she has dropped to help it learn to fly. Marshall says that the grace of God is like this, and he goes on to declare the impartiality of God with regard to "the poor and the rich, the black man and the white."[6] Surely this was nourishing food for the spiritual survival of Georgia slaves.

Such a supportive sense of grace was experienced by Josiah Henson after he awakened to the awful injustice he had wrought on some of his fellow slaves whom he had convoyed through free territory and convinced to return to slavery in the state of Kentucky, to which they had been sent. He did it because, although he had a "sense of right" which was opposed to slavery, he had a "sentiment of honor" about his promise to deliver the slaves to his master's brother. With this sense of honor he withstood the curses of free Blacks, as he left Cincinnati.

Henson later made good his escape, after becoming convinced that there could be no such thing as a "good" master of human slaves, nor any guarantee whatsoever of his ability to carry out good intentions, even if he had them. He allegedly returned from Canada to slave territory many times, to lead slaves to freedom; but he could never forget those he led the other way. The account of the turmoil of his soul expresses an understanding of grace.

Often since that day has my soul been pierced with bitter anguish, at the thought of having been thus instrumental in consigning to the infernal bondage of slavery, so many of my fellow-beings. . . . Having experienced myself the sweetness of liberty, and knowing too well the after-misery of a number of these slaves, my infatuation has often seemed to me to have been the unpardonable sin. But I console myself with the thought that I acted according to my best light, though the light that was in me was darkness. . . . Before God I tried to do my best, and the error of judgement lies at the door of the degrading system under which I had been nurtured.[7]

The key phrase (omitted above) after the first sentence is, "I have wrestled in prayer with God for forgiveness." The very way it is stated bespeaks both a profound awareness of sin and a certitude that the grace of God does apply to such error.

There is still a very strong Black folk faith that even if critical people, Black or White, don't believe in a person's sincerity of purpose and extremes of effort, *God* will "understand and say 'Well done.' " These are the words of a very popular gospel song, and the first line, "If when you give the best of your service," sets off a chain of deep emotions bordering on self-pity by the oppressed and the misunderstood. But the message is nourishing and necessary, especially on such occasions as the funerals of the faithful. It is vital to survival to "be not dismayed when men won't believe you." The purposeful failure to read aright the motives of the oppressed is one way to keep them oppressed. Blacks celebrate the fact that God's grace is the opposite, full of mercy based on understanding of the inner man.

The idea of grace has become so significant in the life and thought of Blacks that it is casually used in ordinary chatter, as a figure of speech. An ex-slave in South Carolina during the Depression spoke of the "old-age pension" she so desperately sought in these terms: "They say its free as de gift of grace from de hand of de Lord."[8]

Grace served the function, from the beginning, of compensating for the absurd, hypercritical, unforgiving world of the slave. Masters had a habit of projecting their own personal frustrations onto their slaves in the form of tongue and even hide lashings. Imaginary infractions were constantly trumped up to keep slaves from getting too "bigitty." The most earnest effort was all too often denounced. All of this accentuated the need for an antidote like grace. It became the means both of affirming the self and of establishing the ultimate acceptability of one's moral efforts. Grace was the means of guaranteeing that the mental cruelty of masters who never gave approval would never succeed in the total destruction of the slave's self-esteem.

The force and effect of grace in such a social context leaves no questions as to why the doctrine was so deeply accepted at folk level. The hymn "Amazing Grace," sung in the Black idiom, is probably the most beloved and moving hymn in the church of the Black masses even today. No mere theological nicety, the grace of God was and is to the Black man a means of life and strength —a source of support and balance and self-certainty in a world whose approval of Blacks is still in extremely short supply.

The most moving tale I encountered in thousands of pages of reading provides the concluding illustration. It involves a funeral remembered in remarkable but understandable detail, after many, many years. An "unlearned" preacher used sound correlation of ideas and brilliant imagination to bring comfort to the survivors of a man who, like "Paul and Silas," had spent time in jail. Almost any Black believer can easily fill in the rest of the details of this description of the proclamation of grace, as recalled by Ned Walker of South Carolina:

Now 'bout Uncle Wash's funeral. Uncle Wash was de blacksmith in de forks of de road 'cross de railroad from Concord Church. He was a powerful man! Him use de hammer and tongs for all de people miles and miles 'round. Him jine de Springvale African Methodist 'Piscopalian Church, but fell from grace. Him covet [stole] a hog of Marse Walt Brice and was sent to de penitentiary for two years, 'bout dat hog. Him contacted consumption down dere and come home. His chest was all sunk in and his ribs full of rheumatism. Him soon went to bed and died. Him was buried on top of de hill, in de pines just north of Woodward. Uncle Pompey preached de funeral. White folks was dere. Marse William was dere, and his nephew, de Attorney General of Arizona. Uncle Pompey took his text 'bout Paul and Silas layin' in jail and dat it was not 'ternally against a church member to go to jail. Him dwell on de life of labor and bravery, in tacklin' kickin' hosses and mules. How him sharpen de dull plow points and make de corn and cotton grow, to feed and clothe de hungry and naked. He look up thru de pine tree tops and say: "I see Jacob's ladder. Brother Wash is climbin' dat ladder. Him is half way up. Ah! Brudders and sisters, pray, while I preach dat he enter in them pearly gates. I see them gates open. Brother Wash done reach de topmost rung in dat ladder. Let us sing wid a shout, dat blessed hymn, 'Dere is a Fountain Filled Wid Blood.'" Wid de first verse de women got to hollerin' and wid de second, Uncle Pompey say: "De dyin' thief [mentioned in the second stanza] I see him dere to welcome Brother Wash in paradise. Thank God! Brother Wash done washed as white as snow and landed safe forever more."

Dat Attorney General turn up his coat in de November wind and say: "I'll be damn!" Marse William smile and 'low: "Oh Tom! Don't be too hard on them. 'Member He will have mercy on them, dat have mercy on others."[9]

Providence of God

Slaves saw a merciful God providentially setting them free. Josiah Henson, whose need for grace has already been seen to be great, projected God's care in smaller but no less providential ways. On an alleged journey as an Underground Railroad conductor he reported God's help several times in rapid sequence. The first example of it was recorded in this expression of indomitable folk belief. "On landing [at Maysville, Kentucky], a wonderful *providence* happened to me. The second person I met in the street was Jefferson Lightfoot, brother of the James Lightfoot . . . who had promised to escape if I would assist them."[10]

En route from Maysville to Cincinnati their boat "sprung a leak before we had got half way, and we narrowly escape being drowned; *providentially,* however, we got to the shore before the boat sunk."[11] When his party arrived, overland, at the Miami River, they were unable to cross over into Cincinnati until assisted by an Exodus-like divine intervention:

This was a great barrier to us, for the water appeared deep, and we were afraid to ask the loan of a boat, being apprehensive it might lead to our detection. We went first up and then down the river, trying to find a convenient crossing-place, but failed. I then said to my company, "Boys, let us go up the river and try again." We started, and after going about a mile we saw a cow coming out of a wood, and going to the river as though she intended to drink. Then said I, "Boys, let us go and see what the cow is about, it may be that she will tell us some news." I said this in order to cheer them up. . . . The cow remained until we approached her within a rod or two; she then walked into the river, and went straight across without swimming, which caused me to remark, "The Lord sent that cow to show us where to cross the river!" This has always seemed to me to be a very wonderful event.[12]

This tendency to see the providence of God in every good experience was virtually universal among slave believers, and very common among all Blacks. Narrative after narrative relates some straw of good fortune in a haystack of adversity, and celebrates it as evidence of the care and concern of the Creator of the universe. An earlier Black scholar, whose name and particular work I have tried unsuccessfully to find once disturbed me greatly with the idea that this Black style of belief was utterly wishful. His work showed, to his own satisfaction and beyond my power to refute, that Black illustrations of providence were highly selective. Black believers exonerated God for unexplainable evil, and praised him for any little good that came their way. Although I could not then successfully rebut this writer, I was fortunate enough to be able to hold my own beliefs about providence. I am now in the interesting position of agreeing with him about the mindset of Blacks, although for totally different reasons.

The quality of life for people is determined by how they read or interpret it. This interpretation, in turn, is revealed in and indeed controlled by how people read reality, human existence, and their Creator. It is not merely wishful to assert and exercise the right to select the portion of one's existence on which one wishes to enlarge, and in which he wishes to spend his time emotionally and spiritually. One of man's inalienable rights is that of locating his own internal living space. It is as if millions of Blacks had declared to the world, "I may work and suffer in this cruel torture chamber which you see and made, but over here, out of your sight and understanding, do I live and move and have my being."

In so doing, Blacks have seized the initiative and determined to emphasize the impact of such small good fortune as has come their way. This habitual accentuation of the positive has maximized the support and strength which they could draw from each instance of God's providence; and this in turn has enabled them to survive in sanity an experience which would have destroyed any other culture and world view long since.

Like grace, this belief in providence supports identity and self-esteem. Gustavus Vassa's 1789 slave narrative states this theme and its effect pointedly. "I believe there are few events in my life which have not happened to many; . . . and, did I consider myself an European, I might say my sufferings were great; but when I compare my lot with that of most of my countrymen [slaves], I regard myself as a *particular favorite of heaven,* and acknowledge the mercies of Providence in every occurrence of my life."[13] Vassa's beginnings as a captured slave boy were retroactively read on this basis. In the instance which follows, his childish fears of clocks and pictures (unseen in his native Africa), and his loneliness, were relieved by the not small fortune of a change of masters.

> On the *African Snow* [a ship], I was called Michael. I had been some time in this miserable, forlorn, and much dejected state, without having anyone to talk to, which made my life a burden, when the kind and unknown hand of the Creator (who in very deed leads the blind in a way they know not) now began to appear, to my comfort; for one day the captain of a merchant ship, called the *Industrious Bee,* came on some business.... While he was at my master's house, it happened that he saw me, and liked me so well that he made a purchase of me."[14]

Vassa's folk doctrine of providence went so far as to cover the weather after a shipwreck (slave ship), in which he was worked unmercifully hard, and badly lacerated, in the process of saving White sailors too drunk and spiritually bankrupt to try to save themselves. Providence received credit for "little" blessings like the sunrise and the subsiding of the swells. "We watched for daylight, and thought every minute an hour until it appeared. At last it saluted our longing eyes, and kind Providence accompanied its approach with what was no small comfort to us, the dreadful swells began to subside; and the next thing we discovered to raise our drooping spirits, was a small key or desolate island."[15]

This positive frame of mind and constant reference to the goodness of God was clearly the ideological descendant of traditional West African faith, which was never conceived in terms of random and impersonal "luck." African world view had always linked good fortune, as well as its reverse (less explicitly), to the gods; and the emphasis unconsciously chosen had always been such as to provide the basis for the celebration of life.

Rev. Wilson Northcross of Alabama illustrated the immediacy of this providential perspective as he recalled his feelings just after he left a group of deserters from the Southern rebel army, having narrowly escaped being murdered.

"All night I prayed to God, and the wives of the men prayed to God for the poor 'nigger,' and also prayed for their cruel husbands. Their prayers prevailed, and I was robbed and let go. I had vowed not to reveal their whereabouts. I left loving God and believing in his providence as I had never believed before."[16] The very fact that the concept of providence rose to Northcross's consciousness at this point is evidence of the view in which he had been steeped. It was the only ideological tool he had with which to comprehend and deal emotionally with his good fortune. Despite all the prior bad fortune that led up to it, there can be little wonder as to why he loved and trusted God the more afterwards. His kind of testimony is still common among Black-culture believers.

There is no way to depress permanently the spirit of a people thus equipped, nor can their total being and drive for life and liberation be suppressed when they refuse ever to consider themselves utterly down and ultimately forsaken. They will always be able to resume the struggle because they will always succeed in seeing somewhere that God is blessing them "right now," even in the darkest hour. No amount of suffering can ever serve as adequate reason for a reading of reality as hopeless. They will bewilder their adversaries because they keep coming and seem never to know when or how to stop, or to accept defeat in life.

It is a great gift, a racial and cultural streak of genius, to be able to "bounce back"; and it comes from a long historical mindset (long before exposure to the Christian faith), amounting almost to an instinct. With bitter humor sharecropper (ex-slave) Manda Walker of South Carolina reported the cynical, cruel abuse of business records by her typically crooked White landlord, as he figured her family's share, after credit purchases. She ended it with the well-known rhyme:

> Naught is naught, and figger is a figger,
> All for de white man, none for de nigger.

But her roots demanded some further word, and she immediately continued thus: "De grave and de resurrection will put everything all right. . . . I have a instinct dat God'll make it all right over and up yonder and dat all our 'flictions will, in de long run, turn out to our 'ternal welfare and happiness."[17]

This instinct of faith was often expressed by a scripture text still very popular and widely quoted among Black believers, which may be rendered: "God works everything together for good to them who love him and answer the call to live by his purposes."[18]

The Holy Spirit

A much more obvious "instinct" among Blackamerican slaves was probably that of possession by deities. The practice of possession or shouting prevailed (and still does) primarily among women of a class oriented to an African culture, and among certain restricted types of Black men. But the belief in the tradition was and is almost universal among Black believers of the masses-oriented churches. In other words, those who are not themselves actively possessed participate vicariously, being strangely moved when others shout. There would be very, very few who would question the authenticity of the shout as evidence of the movement of the Holy Spirit among them, even though many are aware that on occasion the holy overwhelming is faked and/or manipulated.

How this African tradition or "instinct" evolved into a firm Black Protestant doctrine and practice raises some interesting questions. One would be hard pressed for answers were it not for the fact that the confrontation between the cultures and religions, on this very subject, is still taking place, and has been studied by experts within recent years, in Haiti. Sheila Walker reports that Haitian psychiatrist Emerson Douyon found some of the voodoo devotees he tested complaining that they could not get rid of the loas (Haitian parallel to African traditional lesser deities) which occasionally possessed them. They were making the effort in order to climb the social ladder and be identified with a "higher-class" culture. Since possession was already common among voodooist Catholics, it was assumed that Catholicism was useless for purposes of social climbing. The majority Roman faith was already too closely identified with the "lower" classes, and it had failed to free its followers of possession. However, their complaint continued, "if they joined Protestant churches to get away from Voodoo they would then be possessed by the Holy Spirit."[19]

The power and tenacity of the cultural conditioning related to possession is clearly manifest here. It is not the sort of thing that one can shed with ease, and voluntarily. It is, rather, deeply imbedded in the human psyche by subtle and powerfully influential hypnotic and other folk means. It is transmitted and maintained in ways most of which are not planned or conscious, and it is therefore retained involuntarily. In the city where Douyon did his tests, these supposedly primitive possession rites were actually in the process of cultural deemphasis. People were attempting to exercise what is called upward mobility, and to shed "less sophisticated" customs. But the conditioning was irresistible; and it was reinforced by the healing, life-supporting values of the possession tradition, as well as by the fears of retribution from the jilted deities.

That this attempt to shed possession is still at work in the United States among Blacks is evident from an experience in my own ministry, within the decade of the 1960s. A sorority of cosmetologists adjourned their annual meeting to attend our Sunday morning service of worship. The statewide group easily packed our church, and the spirit ran very high. However, oddly, there was no shouting. I learned later that this had been accomplished only by great effort. Several saintly sisters of the beautician trade had restrained themselves by the hardest means, and only temporarily. They had then rushed back to their hotels to shout in the secret sanctity and social safety of their rooms. Some misguided idiot of a nonmember had alleged to them that shouting was not acceptable or at least encouraged at our church. And as sorority members, they didn't want to "disgrace" their group.

The irony of it was that this particular church had an impressive array of authentic shouters ranging from highly placed professionals to pickers of cotton in the immediate neighborhood. Just as equality had prevailed and social distinctions disappeared in traditional African interaction with the gods, so was this church prone to level folk out, or to honor them according to how they responded to God. The difference between them and those of the African tradition was limited to the fact that they had no sacred drum which served to cue in the presence of the gods. For them the fiery presence arrived spontaneously, with no signals from a "baptized" instrument. Rather the Spirit descended as unpredictably as the wind, whose source, as Jesus said, men know not.[20]

Whether one looks at this particular Baptist church or at any one of thousands of other Baptist, Methodist, or Pentecostal churches, the survival and adaptation of this strong, African possession tradition to Christian purposes is obvious. It has been rightly argued that shouting, as such, is neither uniquely nor totally African. Bert Luster of Oklahoma casually supported the idea when he recalled that "niggers and white shouted alike," before the KKK broke up interracial worship.[21] Granted the similarities, two clear qualifications are necessary. One is that crosscultural influences had to be based on roots. The roots of the White frontiersmen's shouting were no doubt in the possession tradition of the Celtic ancestors of the Welsh and Irish Methodists. It had emerged from the collective unconscious of oppressed miners, for instance, in the earliest Welsh revivals. It was brought to the American frontiers by these same people, there to influence ever greater waves of shouting from those in whose psyche the tradition had been even more deeply buried. Blackamerican shouting had its roots in Africa, and the differences between the traditions are not so subtle as to escape easy detection. They relate to the restraint-versus-freedom parameter in much the same way as do the differences between White American social dancing and most Blackamerican social dancing. Where there are contemporary diminutions in difference, they stem from White acculturation to Black, rather than vice versa.

The other qualification of the similarity also relates to the same root-conditioned acculturation process. Diametrically opposed to the thesis of E. Franklin Frazier, it is that the *Blacks adapted their African tradition towards Christianity; not that Blacks took Euro-Christian patterns and changed them towards their own needs. The root continuum is African.* Recognition of this African base underneath Black Christianity's strong doctrinal position and worship tradition regarding the work of the Holy Spirit does not detract from it in the least. In fact Black Christianity is indeed strongest here, as compared to Euro-American Christianity.

This synthesis of African and Christian influences is still resisted, as we have seen, by some Blackamericans, but it was a sound and lasting metamorphosis early accomplished in the American colonies. Those who had once been healingly possessed by a variety of deities were now overshadowed by the one but triune God, in his person as Holy Ghost or Holy Spirit. The music and speech which once induced possession were quite similar to the rhythm repetition, and mass-hypnotic phenomena which accompany much of Blackamerican shouting even today. However, without such presumptions of psychic cause and effect, and despite their implications, enslaved Africans early concluded that they could rightly term their possession tradition Christian. They used this spiritual "transplant" from Africa, with a few changes of terminology and a few strategic modifications, to perpetuate on a vast scale both the African-American religious tradition and a vitalized Christianity. This, I contend, was the single most brilliant and productive adaptation of all the numerous adaptations of African religion into Black Christianity.

Before considering the modifications necessary to accomplish this transition, it may be well briefly to review the process whereby a variety of African religions and cultures had fused into what could become so useful and universal a Blackamerican religious tradition. Bastide[22] has shown how the Yoruba family (including Dahomean) and Ashanti-related cultures evolved toward domination of Black culture in specific New World localities because of their superior numbers. It may also be said, in connection with the doctrine of the Holy Spirit, that this dominance occurred because of superior ability to cope with an oppressed existence. For these reasons, it is possible to trace the more prominent features of these two cultures, and especially the Yoruba-related traditions of possession, as seen in Bahia (Brazil), Haiti, Cuba, Trinidad, and, in a more diluted state, in Black U.S.A.

The modifications required involved concepts of monotheism/ polytheism and immanence/transcendence, as applied to the possessing deity(ies), and more mundane concerns such as the function and content of possession, and the role and status of the possessed. We have already said that Blacks evolved an understanding that the plurality of beings which had formerly possessed them were in fact only one, and that this one was none other than the third person of the Trinity, the Holy Spirit or Holy Ghost.[23] The shift to a single God was undoubtedly influenced by strong White witness at the theoretical level, against polytheism. But the often unconscious preachments and judgments by Whites in favor of monotheism would not have been so effective had it not been for the African concept of one High God. Grafted to this historic root was the superior functioning of a single deity as existentially encountered by the slaves both in the experience of possession and in the need for an overarching single principle to bring life-supporting order out of an absurdly cruel world.

This monotheistic modification required more than a radical, numerical reduction in the pantheon of deities. It also necessitated a major revision of the esteem in which the Possessor was held. He, being now the one God, was not to be thought of as just another member of a large and often competitive and manipulable group of lesser deities. The concept was a move back toward transcendence, but here transcendence was applied to a condition that *needed* transcending: slavery.

The deviation from the earlier African ideas of the utter transcendence and ineffability of God has already been mentioned as Christianity's chief new contribution to Black belief. And this new and supportive immanence of God has been seen to have been convincingly perceived by the slave as it was expressed in the possession experience. There were, of course, other ways short of outright possession in which the divine presence and guidance were perceived and experienced, in worship and otherwise. But ecstasy, once evidence of the presence and possession of lesser deities, became the crucial bridge between the natural and the supernatural or ultimate. Shouting Black folk gained a kind of transcendence over their degraded slave condition, even as God was now seen to be "Immanuel," God *with* us. The trinitarian dogma, developed out of utterly different cultural roots and intellectual requirements, had thus providentially prepared room for personal relations with the godhead, not unlike the previous possessors in polytheism. In some places, Catholics went a step further and preserved the divine plurality by identifying the saints with the lesser deities. The Church itself, of course, did not approve of this, but the adaptive instinct, noting the match in the traditions, would not be dissuaded.

The name by which the possessing Spirit was referred to in direct address, however, was the second person of the Trinity, according to his earthly or human name, Jesus. Nowhere was the doctrine of God's immanence more evident than in the folksy way slaves talked to Jesus. Mystical communication was most often with "Jesus," with distress frequently calling forth a "Have mercy, Lawd!" Even here the reference was to the Lord Jesus; and the titles God and Jesus were virtually interchangeable in other kinds of address. Slaves soon excelled their masters even in talk *about* Jesus, so that he was both a common topic of conversation and a common spiritual presence. Their ancient traditions of communication with the living dead made this talking with Jesus easy. Perhaps it became a good substitute for the chats they could no longer conceive of having with ancestors on the other side of the Atlantic.

The resurrection and continuing presence of Jesus was not in the least surprising to the African mind; the real shocker was the Incarnation—that *High God* should have come to dwell among men, first in human flesh, and then by his Spirit. This strange and wonderful news was joyously embraced, however, and the Holy Spirit became the agent whereby Blacks personally experienced that Incarnated Presence in the world. Some were possessed outright, and others were blessed simply by knowing that the Spirit had "come by here." As had always been the case, some were dramatically possessed and some were not, but all were blessed. Some were possessed only occasionally, and some were overcome regularly. Some spoke of the experience in traditional Christian terms, and many others simply thought of themselves as Christians and took part regularly in shouting. Whatever the time or the terminology, the once distant deity was now the Possessor.

One of the most interesting accounts to come out of the Civil War is Col. Thomas Wentworth Higginson's record of his experiences with his regiment of ex-slave volunteers. They often referred to themselves as the "gospel army," and no White officer could match (or needed to) their own folk habit of sermonizing on the will of God for their lives. Except when in battle or otherwise on duty, some of these hardened and heroic men held a "shout" each and every night until curfew. Willing and even anxious to shed their blood to wipe out slavery, their morale was sustained by their unashamed nightly engagement in an Afro-Christian rite leading to a ritualized possession, the "ring shout."[24]

Quite obviously there was no avoiding the fact that the new understandings of the Holy Spirit as Possessor required drastic alterations in the content of some types of the possession experience. Sheila Walker contends that the previous African tradition of possession, in which one assumed the attributes of the gods, revealed the gods' character or personality to be either a reenactment of a highly enjoyable previous stage of life, or a projection of a highly desirable future state.[25] All this was potentially very therapeutic, as we shall see; but its transparent dependence on people, at best, and its susceptibility to conscious manipulation, at worst, made the old tradition appear to be in need of more transcendence. The tendency away from the more personally oriented specifics robbed the new possession of the old and more healing capacity to engage in ritualized expression/disclosure, fitted to the individual's needs. No longer was there a tailor-made deity facilitating catharsis, and, of course, almost never was there a priest or adept to match specialized deities to individual people's needs.

Prayerful supplications were still made for blessings such as freedom, but the Holy Spirit was not, as Possessor, asked to do the mundane chores once assigned to lesser deities. The pragmatic move away from deities who did not deliver became a thing of the past. The Holy Spirit simply possessed people ecstatically, and gave them the inner strength and self-affirmation to survive. He also was known to backstop the traditional herbal and other cures, and, on occasion, to heal outright. Above all, he made people "happy," a term which came to be synonymous with possession, from the slightest beginnings of the experience to the outright shout.

A Texas centenarian put it: "De spirit jes' come down out de sky and you forgits all your troubles."[26] Another Texan reported. "One of the slaves was a sort-a preacher and sometimes Marster 'lowed him to preach to the niggers, but he have to preach with a tub over his head, 'cause he git so happy he talk too loud."[27] A sister from Alabama became a "foot-washin' Baptist" just after she was emancipated, but there was no such church near where she lived when interviewed. She asserted her old ways wherever she went. "I jes goes wid de udder Baptis' en sets in de amen corner, en iffen I wants to shout, I shouts, en nobody ain't gonna stop me, bless de lord!"[28]

Nobody had better try to stop her. That came soon to be a matter of resisting the Holy Spirit's free activity, and a kind of mortal sin, therefore. An ancient ex-slave in Charleston, known to my wife in her childhood, reported: "I goes to chu'ch when I kin an' sing too, but if I sing an' it doan mobe me any, den dat a sin on de Holy Ghost."[29] An elderly Texas saint summed it up: "I still shouts at meetin's. I don't have nothin' to do with it. It hits me jes' like a streak of lightnin', and there ain't no holdin' it. I goes now to meetin's and tries to 'have, but when I gets the spirit, I just can't hold that shoutin' back. The young folks makes fun of me, but I don't mind. Style am crowded all the grace out of 'ligion today."[30]

Possession in the African tradition was the height of worship —the supreme religious act. Without conscious memory of the tradition as such, and without any special rationale save that of the "happy" impact of possessions, this view was continued by American Blacks. Though this last slave statement accurately reports a widespread assault of less expressive "style" against this tradition, it is alive and thriving today among the churches of today's Blackamerican masses. These constitute the vast majority of believing Blacks. Further, there is a return towards a deep awareness of the personal work of the Holy Spirit among some culture-and-religion-conscious young Black intellectuals. A good illustration of this may be seen in the African Methodist Episcopal church near Harvard University.

The persistence of the view of possession as the climax of worship is of more than mere cultural tenacity. Despite the less specific catharsis, as compared to that of the African tradition, Black worship does provide a ritualized means of important emotional release. The nonspecificity of the current catharsis has the value of requiring less personal and therefore less threatening disclosure. This works well with the low-trust levels and the attempts at emotional self-sufficiency necessary for survival in a society that is still basically hostile to Blacks. Even the once intimate and supportive extended Black family is now inclined to be prey to the common estrangement of urban life. The climactic worship experience of direct or vicarious possession serves well the needs of modern Blacks.

Phrasing it another way, the worship of the Black masses provides the atmosphere of freedom in which the Holy Spirit can do his confidential work within every person, just as he will. The encouragement of individual response is, in itself, healing to identity. The deep respect maintained for everyone's expression is likely to be the most accepting and unrestrictedly affirming experience in the life of the Black believer. Over and above this, God accepts these overflows of feeling and, indeed, generates them to his praise. However culturally conditioned the scholars may prove these responses to be, they are soundly perceived by Blacks to be absolutely free and uninhibited. Thus God's acceptance of a person's shouting as worship is the other side of the coin of God's acceptance and love of the usually concealed real person who is worshiping. This person must be hidden almost everywhere else. The ecstasy of being somebody-to-the-hilt, indwelt by the presence of God himself, is nourishment enough to keep a despised and oppressed Black person courageous and creative for at least another week.

This process has, on occasion, been criticized as escapism, but the real escapists are the suicides and the drug addicts, who refuse to maintain the struggle to be and to deal with life. Without the strength of the empowering presence of the Holy Spirit, Black people would have had to surrender in the struggle for existence long ago. Because of this strength they can "take" more, but they can also keep cool and "dish out" more, in their own defense and for their own liberation.

In all candor, however, it must be stated that the Black church does not have a monopoly on this kind of strength. The African possession tradition survives in Black culture outside the church's institutional trappings. This truth is much more obvious today than it was forty years ago, now that Black gospel music is both highly accepted and clearly related to the Black music of the entertainment world. The plain fact is that some form of ecstatic possession has always been present in the branch of African culture roots which surfaced in the jazz world. And the communal creativity of an instrumental, vocal, or dance "soul session" in a night club still has some of the same creative possibilities for human healing that a church service might have. What is thought of religiously as "freedom of (or in) the spirit" is an altered state of consciousness which, while closely associated with the Holy Spirit, also has a fairly close parallel in the "secular" context of jazz. The same kinds of psychophysical phenomena such as music, rhythm, and movement help in the achievement of the state of consciousness in both cases. Religious and jazz forms of possession are based on the same African-influenced cultural expectations. That there are similarities between Black jazz and church music, and that the crossover between them has been restored should come as no surprise whatever. A Black Baptist preacher's daughter named Aretha Franklin can "get loose" and celebrate as well in one context as the other. The deeply religious feelings evoked by Roberta Flack's rendition of the hymn "Come, Ye Disconsolate" are not one whit less religious just because the hymn is recorded on a "jazz" album.

Consciously or unconsciously, all African culture is deeply religious and celebrative, as well as involved in the material concerns of human existence. This refusal to engage in the Western world's dichotomy of flesh or the material on the one hand, and soul or spirit on the other, is one more reason for the helping and healing power of the Holy Spirit tradition in the Black church.

Describing this dichotomy Sheila Walker states:

Much Christian worship is characterized by humility, effacement, and the silence of the body. The activity of the body is suspended in conformity to the dualistic metaphysic which separates mind and body and condemns the body to effacement as the mind communes with God. . . . The Christian bodily techniques are opposed point for point to those of the possession cults of the African and Afro-American groups in question. . . . The African gods only live in the measure to which they are reincarnated in the *flesh* [italics mine] of their devotees, . . . when the ritual becomes a living, sacred mythology."[31]

Walker studied Brazilians and Haitians, but Holy Spirit possession of U.S.A. Blacks is also African in body response.

Some recent "drawing-board culture" experiments in worship among Whites have sought to restore "primitive" unity of the person. But the great strength of Black Christianity is that in its worship it never abandoned the wholism of the African tradition, nor bowed the knee of conformity to sterile White canons of religious expression. What Walker rightly considers to be the strengths of the African-based religious traditions of Brazil and Haiti have been preserved also in the Blackamerican religious tradition, all unaware of the supporting rationale provided now by stimulating research.

Walker also describes the profound therapeutic values of African worship, possession, and celebration. Again, what she says applies also to the Blackamerican tradition, with the previously noted exception that one no longer responds to a god fitted to his own characteristics.

In the aesthetically satisfying atmosphere of joy and festivities, suppressed and repressed aspects of the personality come to the fore in symbolic, socially approved form. This is an important element in maintaining both social and individual equilibrium. In possession the individual may free himself of conflicts, complexes, and hidden tendencies in dancing for the god whose characteristics are in some way analogous to his own. Instead of the seemingly flat and incomplete technique of trying to express one's unconscious self only verbally while lying on an analyst's couch isolated from society, the possessed individual expresses himself with his whole body through drama and dance in a situation involving many of the people with whom he normally interacts.[32]

Over against this healing efficacy one challenge often advanced is that of the safety of the possessed—his role and responsibility in its maintenance if he is indeed overshadowed. African tradition held that if a person was hurt, it was punishment from the god(s). Accepted as such, often with well-founded assumptions as to the causative offense, the "bad trip" or injurious possession was still beneficial. Blackamerican Christianity has developed a contrasting faith that God's presence is *always* healing. I myself have to hold it to be true, having spent more than fifty years in shouting services without ever seeing a person hurt. Some witnesses are frequently and severely scared; but I have seen even the "lateral pass" (football vintage) of a small infant executed flawlessly, with no injury to the shouting young mother (who sailed over a pew) or to the baby thus unceremoniously committed to the care of a nearby relative.

The explanation for this "safety record" involves more than the undeniable and constant benevolence of the Holy Spirit as Possessor. There is also a cultural conditioning which for centuries has given over to the possession experience only a subsystem of the total ego, both in Africa and in the Americas. The ego always regulates its capacity to regress in its own service, and people always "keep enough sense" not to get hurt or to hurt others. As Walker says, it is "terminable under emergency conditions by the subject unaided," and it is "subject to occurrence only when the individual judges circumstances to be safe."[33]

I can personally testify to the validity of this statement and its applicability to Blackamerican religion. Years ago I was found shouting in the baptismal pool, having just completed the immersion of a series of eleven which began with our youngest daughter and ended with our youngest son. It is understandable that I should have been "half happy" from the start, and that I should have gone all the way into unspeakable ecstasy when the son made an unusually firm, creative statement just before he was immersed. He was only eight. Seeing my blessed condition an usher at the top of the pool stairs (not dressed for water) became alarmed for fear I would drown or otherwise hurt myself. When he sought to restrain me and lost his balance, things swiftly shifted from the sublime to the ludicrous; and I returned to normalcy in a split second, in plenty of time to prevent him from ruining his "Sunday-go-to-meetin'" suit.

Such standby reserves of control, although almost never openly discussed, prevail throughout the Blackamerican Church. And rather than operating against the authenticity of the possession experience, they facilitate entry and freedom by the safety which they provide, making it easier to dare to be possessed. Even in the Pentecostal tradition, where there appears to be an elaborate system of conventions that govern the onset and termination of a kind of mass shout or dance, the existence of the signal system amounts to a cultural conditioning that retains the genuineness of the experience while controlling its duration.

In neither Africa nor Afro-America has possession ever been considered to be an illness. Rather it has been thought of as the supreme as well as the most dramatic aspect of worship. Even if a person was known to be disturbed mentally, the possession itself was not thought of as a symptom. This arose out of the African view of pathological behavior inside possession as a form of controlled outlet. Thus the possessing deity was not exorcised and driven out. After all he had come and taken possession in order to help.[34]

This contrasts with the nonritualized, nonsocialized possession experiences recorded in the New Testament. These possessions involved demonic and undesirable possessors who had to be driven out. Even when the possessed, in African tradition, is acting out the deepest libidinal conflicts such as sexual, he is doing it in the presence of the gods and in healthy combination with other symbolic expressions. Access is thus gained to repressed material not otherwise available,[35] and solutions or resolutions often achieved. The same occurs occasionally in Black Christian possessions, but I am sorry to report that it is virtually all *sub rosa*. Nobody would dare confess a healing sexual climax as a part of worship, no matter how many times it might occur. The one place I know of where sexual climax takes place "for the record" is in the Father Divine sect, whose sexually segregated devotees are led in "vibrations" which are surely calculated both to "praise Father" and to relieve the inescapable tensions of this ascetic life style.

Another contrast between Blackamerican and Afro-American practices of the more traditional, pre-Christian types arises out of the growing American erasure of social distinctions among those desiring and not desiring possession, a factor already alluded to. It is predictable that the recovery of the tradition by Blackamerican intellectuals will sooner or later be paralleled in the Caribbean and Brazil. There the present state would seem to be one in which only the socially and economically dispossessed yearn for spiritual possession. On the other hand, it has long been true that cultural conditioning for possession among Blackamericans has not necessarily followed economic class lines. Some have been wealthy and/or well educated. Walker has advanced a model for explaining this in more detail than just saying that "the Lord blessed the faithful shouter." She suggests that it takes a *stronger* ego to yield in faith to possession, with no more than a small percentage of people shouting from compulsive and pathological need.

This stronger-ego theory meshes with the Blackamerican folk belief that at least some people are, without any social deprivation, simply born with a predisposition to shout. It may be that their mothers' shouting increased their cultural conditioning. On the other hand, the permissive community of faith has recognized that others have appropriately sensed the genuine and deep movement of the Holy Spirit within them without shouting, giving evidence by the shedding of tears or the swaying of the head, or some other personal expression. The one rigid tenet of Black faith in this regard is that when the Spirit deeply touches one, he will do something visible, no matter how subtle. To repress this evidence is to "squelch the Spirit" and sin against the Holy Ghost.

The presence of a wide variety of socioeconomic backgrounds among shouters in the Black church should not conceal the fact that a great many Black churches in which shouting does *not* take place have congregations with higher income levels and more formal education. A good explanation for their lower shouting averages emerges from a possible parallel to an African analysis: "A person who has no serious difficulties in the course of life may never be called upon to ask whether or not he is properly serving his gods. He may never be placed in a situation in which possession would be necessary as a release.[36]

Privileged Blacks do not all follow this pattern, of course. I have seen the school superintendent of a major African city deeply involved in the life and work of a Spiritualist (Pentecostal-type) church. Important political figures in my own American experience have also been caught up and happy in a supposedly "primitive" possession tradition.

It is fascinating to note that the trance dances characteristic of traditional African religious possession are not unlike the "holy dance" of the modern Pentecostal and other Blackamerican churches. In fact, a strong influence from Blackamerican Pentecostals is sweeping Black African Christianity, bringing back to the Black churches of that continent the indigenous expressions so long suppressed by White missionaries. It is only accurate to say that this same suppression happened, Black on Black, in the early days of the Black church in America. We have seen earlier that the venerable African Methodist Episcopal bishop, Daniel Payne, attempted to suppress the clearly African "ring shout" in Maryland. Even this possession pattern was constricted in concession to White Puritanism. We are only now coming to a healthy understanding of the strengths which have possessed Blacks and brought them safe thus far.

At last we can say, with suitable sophistication, that possessed individuals are actualizing themselves rather than denying themselves, on "a plane of reality more powerful, sacred, and meaningful than the everyday." In a world in which even African Blacks in countries governed by themselves, are subject to exploitation and a gross imbalance of the world's goods and power, "ritual possession, rather than destroying the integrity of the self [like much of the rest of reality], provides an increased scope for fulfillment."[37]

While Western Christian mysticism is individualistic and escapist, producing hermits and fierce, strict, ascetic holy men and revival preachers, Black tradition of involvement with the Holy Spirit is gregarious, collective, and celebrative. It is built on group solidarity, and impossible without the cultural conditioning, support, and dialogue of the believing Black community.

This conditioning is no mere figment of theory, even though the stimulating work of social anthropologist Sheila Walker has done much to help me see and form this very analysis. Rather, Black traditional responses and insights amount to a set of deep convictions which plainly provide balance and perspective and healing. Walker reports that "in most traditional areas where religious beliefs and practices continue to carry conviction, religion is the cultural system par excellence by means of which conflict resolution is achieved."[38]

If, as Paul suggested, the fruits of the work of the Holy Spirit include love, joy, peace, long-suffering, and faith,[39] then the Black-church tradition of the Holy Spirit has much to commend it. Among Blackamerican believers the Holy Spirit is interchangeable with a love that "flows from heart to heart and breast to breast," establishing group support, identity, and solidarity. This is love at its highest. The fruit of joy is perhaps never excelled, as the Black church celebrates the goodness of God despite a life of deprivation. The fruit of peace is easily translated to mean the inward peace and healing that we have referred to so many times, whether in theological or therapeutic terms. The fruit of long-suffering is unmistakable in the capacity of Blacks to endure what surely would have driven others to suicide long ago. And who has more of the fruit of faith, more of a capacity to see and know the providence of God in the deepest of suffering and sorrow? I am forced to contend that the Black tradition is the all-time champion producer of the fruits of the work of the Holy Spirit. All other academic or theological consideration of the subject is suspect of irrelevancy unless and until it can approach this track record.

A Concluding Word

It is obvious that God has providentially employed the African roots and the Christian exposure of Blackamericans, together with their overall experience, to forge a religious tradition of surpassing power and profound truth. It is far beyond what most people, Black or White, including myself, have customarily assumed it to be, even though we may have held the tradition in high esteem. It is also obvious that what I have done in this book only scratches the surface. My own research has yielded reams, as it were, of research on the topics treated and on many others, to report which would only have rendered this work unwieldily long. It would also have demanded far more time to complete than was possible. I have had to resign myself to the fact that I cannot even now say all that I know, and there is far more of this body of Black belief that I have not touched in any way. I can only hope that what I have said will stimulate further study, from a perspective that I hope will be changed by the ideas that I have shared here. I am particularly anxious to see more work done on the subject of the folk christology among Blacks, a subject I have dealt with only slightly, under the topic of "The Holy Spirit."

Notes

Introduction

1. Gayraud S. Wilmore, *Black Religion and Black Radicalism* (Garden City, N.Y.: Doubleday, 1972), p. 301.

2. W. E. B. DuBois, *The Negro* (1915; reprint ed., New York: Oxford University Press, 1970), pp. 113–114.

3. DuBois, *The World and Africa* (New York: International Publishers, 1946), pp. xi–xii.

4. Sterling D. Plumpp, *Black Rituals* (Chicago: Third World Press, 1972), p. 99. Bishop Turner, of the African Methodist Episcopal church, was a great political leader and Black nationalist, as well as a great church builder during the golden era of the Black church after the Civil War.

1. The Setting

1. John W. Blassingame, *The Slave Community* (New York: Oxford University Press, 1972), pp. 17–18.

2. Thomas Wentworth Higginson, *Army Life in a Black Regiment* (1869; reprint ed., Boston: Beacon Press, 1962) pp. 17–18.

3. Jourdan Anderson, "To My Old Master," in *The Black Experience,* ed. Frances S. Freedman (New York: Bantam Books, 1970), p. 99.

2. The African-American Linkage

1. Wilmore, *Black Religion and Black Radicalism,* p. 4.

2. Roger Bastide, *African Civilizations in the New World* (New York: Harper & Row, 1971).

3. Joseph H. Washington, Jr., *Black Sects and Cults* (Garden City, N.Y.: Doubleday, 1972), pp. 97, 84.

4. Yosef ben Jochannan, *African Origins of the Major "Western Religions"* (New York: Alkebu-Lan Books, 1970). Address: 209 W. 125th Street, Suite 204, New York, N.Y.

5. Washington, *Black Sects and Cults,* p. 24.

6. George P. Rawick, *The American Slave: A Composite Autobiography,* vol. 1: *From Sundown to Sunup* (Westport, Conn.: Greenwood Publishing Co., 1972), pp.

7. Galatians 3:11.

8. DuBois, *The Negro,* p. 21

9. James Boyd Christensen, "The Adaptive Functions of Fanti Priesthood," *Continuity and Change in African Cultures,* ed. W. R. Bascom and M. J. Herskovits (Chicago: University of Chicago Press, 1959), p. 262, 276.

10. Ibid. p. 274.

11. Isaac O. Delano, *Owe L'Esin Oro: Yoruba Proverbs—Their Meaning and Usage* (Ibadan, Nigeria: Oxford University Press, 1966), pp. 99, 129, 122.

12. R. Sutherland Rattray, *Ashanti Proverbs* (Oxford: Clarendon Press, 1914), pp. 34, 35, 33, 31.

13. Christensen, "Fanti Priesthood," p. 266.

14. Newbell Niles Puckett, *The Magic and Folk Beliefs of the Southern Negro* (1926; reprint ed., New York: Dover Publications, 1969), pp. 561–562, 526.

15. Ibid., p. 566.

16. Rawick, *American Slave,* vol. 2, pt. 1, p. 69; vol. 3, pt. 3, p. 12.

17. Ibid., vol. 1, pp. 39–41.

18. Ibid., vol. 1, p. 31.

19. Wilmore, *Black Religion and Black Radicalism,* pp. 37–38.

20. Harvey Cox, *The Seduction of the Spirit* (New York: Simon and Schuster, 1973), p. 117.

21. Puckett, *Folk Beliefs,* pp. 467–471.

22. Ibid., pp. 132–133; 147.

23. Washington, *Black Sects and Cults,* p. 24.

24. Carter G. Woodson, *The History of the Negro Church* (3rd ed.; Washington, D.C.: Associated Publishers, 1972), p. 7.

25. E. Franklin Frazier, *The Negro Church in America,* (New York: Schocken Books, 1963) p. 6. Cf. P. Mercier, "The Fon of Dahomey," in *African Worlds,* ed. Daryll Forde (London: Oxford University Press, 1954), p. 234.

26. John S. Mbiti, *African Religions and Philosophy* (New York: Praeger, 1969), p. 234.

27. Lawrence N. Jones, "They Sought a City: The Black Church and Churchmen in the Nineteenth Century," *Union Seminary Quarterly Review* XXVI (Spring 1971): 258.

28. See chapter 1, pp. 7–8.

29. Mbiti, *African Religions,* p. 275.

30. Washington, *Black Sects and Cults,* p. 35.

31. Frazier, *Negro Church,* pp. 8–9.

32. Winthrop S. Hudson, "Shouting Methodists," *Encounter* 29,1:82–83.

33. Christensen, "Fanti Priesthood," p. 258.

34. Charles Spencer Smith, *A History of the African Methodist Episcopal Church,* vol. 2 (Philadelphia: Book Concern of the A.M.E. Church, 1922; reprint ed. New York: Johnson Reprint Corporation, 1968), pp. 126–127.

35. Ernest Borneman, "The Roots of Jazz," in *Jazz,* ed. Nat Hentoff and A. J. McCarthy (New York: Rinehart, 1959), p. 21; cited by LeRoi Jones, *Blues People* (New York: William Morrow, 1963), p. 42.

36. *Webster's New International Dictionary* (Springfield, Mass.: G & C Merriam Co., 1927), p. 843.

37. Puckett, *Folk Beliefs,* p. 7.

38. Bastide, *African Civilizations,* pp. 11–12.

39. Puckett, *Folk Beliefs,* p. 553.

40. Ibid., p. 545.

41. Ibid.

42. Ibid., p. viii.

43. Ibid., pp. 520–521.

44. Ibid., p. 573.

45. Ibid., pp. 573–575.

46. Ibid., pp. 8–9.

47. Ibid., p. 33.

48. Ibid., pp. 530–540.

49. Sheila S. Walker, *Ceremonial Spirit Possession in Africa and Afro-America* (Leiden: E. J. Brill, 1972), pp. 86–87.

50. Maya Deren, *Divine Horsemen: The Voodoo Gods of Haiti* (New York: Chelsea House, 1970), pp. 188–200, 248, 320–321.

51. Frederick Douglass, *Narrative of the Life and Times of Frederick Douglass, An American Slave*, ed. Benjamin Quarles (Cambridge, Mass.: Harvard University Press, 1960), pp. 101–103.

52. Puckett, *Folk Beliefs,* pp. 174–175. Cf. Christensen, p. 266.

53. Wilmore, *Black Religion and Black Radicalism,* p. 19.

55. Ibid., pp. 20 and 28–29.

3. The African Roots of American Black Belief

1. Mbiti, *African Religions,* p. xi.

2. Ibid., p. 2.

3. Ibid., p. 2.

4. LeRoi Jones, *Blues People,* pp. 6–7.

5. E. Bolaji Idowu, "Introduction," in *Biblical Revelation and African Beliefs,* ed. Kwesi A. Dickson and Paul Ellingworth (Maryknoll, N.Y.: Orbis Books, 1969), p. 16.

6. Stephan N. Ezeanya, "God, Spirits and the Spirit World," in *Biblical Revelation and African Beliefs,* p. 16.

7. Mbiti, "Christianity and Traditional Religions in Africa," *International Review of Mission* LIX, 236 (October 1970):435.

8. Ibid.

9. Ibid.

10. Ibid.

11. Carl G. Jung, *Psychology and Religion* (New Haven: Yale University Press, 1938), p. 58.

12. Ezeanya, "God, Spirits," pp. 35–36.

13. Idowu, *Olodumare God in Yoruba Belief* (London: Longman Group Limited, 1962), pp. 20–22.

14. Mbiti, *Concepts of God in Africa* (New York: Praeger, 1970), p. 120.

15. John 1:3.

16. J. B. Danquah, *The Akan Doctrine of God* (London: Frank Cass & Co., Ltd., 1968), p. 193.

17. Mbiti, *Concepts of God,* p. 150.

18. Ibid.

19. *Larouse World Mythology,* ed. Pierre Grimal, trans. Patricia Beardsworth (New York: G. P. Putnam, 1965), p. 531.

20. Geoffrey Parrinder, *African Mythology* (London: Paul Hamlyn, 1967), p. 20.

21. Richard F. Burton, *Wit and Wisdom From West Africa,* vol. 5 in *Afro America Studies* (1865; New York: New American Library, 1969), p. xviii.

22. Ibid., pp. 414–436.

23. K. A. Busia, "Ashanti," *African Worlds,* ed. Daryll Forde (London: Oxford University Press, 1954), p. 206.

24. Rattray, *Ashanti Proverbs,* p. 20.

25. Ibid., p. 21.

26. G. W. Sannes, *African "Primitives": Function and Form in African Masks and Figures,* trans. Margaret King (New York: Africana Publishing Corporation, 1970), pp. 24–32.

27. *Larouse,* p. 531. Cf. Gen. 36:8.

28. ben Jochannan, *African Origins,* pp. 50, x.

29. Adebayo Adesanya, "Yoruba Metaphysical Thinking," *Odu* nos. 4–6 (1957–1958):38–41. Cf. Pierre Verger, "The Yoruba High God," *Odu* 2,2 (January 1966):38–41.

30. Samuel Crowther, *Yoruba Grammar* (1852), quoted in Burton, *Wit and Wisdom,* pp. xix–xxi.

31. Rattray, *Ashanti Proverbs,* pp. 19–20.

32. Ibid. Also, Danquah, *Akan Doctrine of God,* pp. 55, 198–206.

33. Idowu, "Introduction," pp. ix–xxv.

34. Idowu, *Olodumare,* pp. 36–45. Cf. J. Olumide Lucas, *The Religion of the Yorubas* (Lagos, Nigeria: C.M.S. Bookshop, 1948), p. 34, and Verger, "Yoruba High God," pp. 30–32.

35. Ezeanya, "God, Spirits," p. 42.

36. Idowu, *Olodumare,* pp. 80–85.

37. Ezeanya, "God, Spirits," p. 46.

38. Acts 17:24–25.

39. Carol Tavris, "Magic & Medicine, A Sketch of Thomas Lambo," *Psychology Today,* February 1972, p. 65.

40. Danquah, *Akan Doctrine,* p. 189.

41. Robin Horton, "Conference: 'The High God in Africa,'" *Odu* 2, 2 (January 1966):88.

42. Ezeanya, "God, Spirits," p. 41.

43. Washington, *Black Sects and Cults,* p. 30.

44. John Beattie and John Middleton, ed., "Introduction," *Spirit Medi-*

umship and Society in Africa (New York: Africana Publishing Corporation, 1969), p. xxi.

45. Idowu, *Olodumare,* p. 41.

46. Burton, *Wit and Wisdom,* p. 441. From this point onward, the book source of the proverbs will not be noted. *Wit and Wisdom* has been a source for proverbs of the Yoruba, Efik of Calabar, Ga of Accra, Wolof of Senegal, and the Ashanti Twi.

Other Yoruba sources are Delano's *Yoruba Proverbs,* Adesanya's "Yoruba Metaphysical Thinking," and Ruth Finnegan's *Oral Literature in Africa* (Oxford: Clarendon Press, 1970).

Other Ashanti sources are Rattray's *Ashanti Proverbs* and Danquah's *Akan Doctrine of God.* The source for the Gonja proverbs, also from Ghana, is C. S. Kponkpogori, C. J. Natomaj, and O. Rytz, *Gonja Proverbs,* ed. O. Rytz Local Studies Series, no. 3 (Legon, Ghana: Institute of African Studies, 1966).

47. Phil. 4:11.

48. Rattray, *Ashanti Proverbs,* p. 50.

49. Idowu, *Olodumare,* p. 175.

50. Ibid., pp. 171–185.

51. Delano, *Yoruba Proverbs,* p. 15.

52. Washington, *Black Sects and Cults,* pp. 20–21.

53. Rom. 8:28.

54. Ezeanya, "God, Spirits," p. 45.

55. Deut. 32:35. Cf. Ps. 94:1; Jer. 51:36; and Rom. 12:19.

56. Delano, *Yoruba Proverbs,* p. 87; Musa Gotom, Anga (Northern Nigeria) doctoral candidate, School of Theology, Claremont, California.

57. Mentioned in Burton, *Wit and Wisdom,* p. 201.

58. Ezeanya, "God, Spirits," pp. 37–38.

59. Idowu, *Olodumare,* p. 5.

60. Gal. 6:7.

61. Matt. 10:26; Luke 12:2.

62. Matt. 5:45.

63. Deut. 8:3.

64. Luke 6:29.

65. Submitted by Musa Gotom (see n. 56).

4. Generation of Meaning in Black America

1. Rawick, *American Slave,* vol. 7, part 2, p. 75.

2. Incomplete copy of manuscript of Fisk University Social Science

Research Institute, "Unwritten History of Slavery," 1929–1930, p. iii. Now published as Rawick, *The American Slave,* vol. 18.

3. Rawick, *American Slave,* vol. 3, part 4, p. 159.

4. Ibid., vol. 1, *From Sundown to Sunup.*

5. Ibid., vol. 2, part 1, p. 91.

6. Ibid., vol. 3, part 4, p. 192.

7. Fisk University, "Unwritten History," p. 47.

8. Luke 16:19–31.

9. Price M. Cobbs and William H. Grier, *The Jesus Bag* (New York: McGraw-Hill, 1971), p. 164.

10. Rawick, *American Slave,* vol. 2, part 2, pp. 158–159.

11. Ibid., vol. 7, part 2, p. 24.

12. Fisk University, "Unwritten History," pp. 297, 299.

13. Rawick, *American Slave,* vol. 5, part 2, p. 117.

14. Ibid., vol. 4, part 2, p. 135.

15. Ibid., vol. 2, part 2, pp. 184–185.

16. Ibid., vol. 5, part 2, pp. 68–69.

17. Ibid., vol. 3, part 4, p. 82.

18. Ibid., vol. 4, part 2, p. 199.

19. Ibid., vol. 7, part 2, p. 173.

20. Ibid., p. 6.

21. Ibid., vol. 3, part 4, p. 255.

22. Ibid., vol. 7, part 1, p. 37.

23. William Craft, "Running a Thousand Miles for Freedom," in *Great Slave Narratives,* ed. Arna Bontemps (Boston: Beacon Press, 1969), pp. 288–289.

24. J. W. C. Pennington, "The Fugitive Blacksmith," in *Great Slave Narratives,* ed. Bontemps, p. 237.

25. Pennington, "The Fugitive Blacksmith," pp. 254–255.

26. Gustavus Vassa, "The Life of Gustavus Vassa, the African," *Great Slave Narratives,* ed. Bontemps, p. 62.

27. Rawick, *American Slave,* vol. 3, part 4, p. 66.

28. Alexander Glennie, *Sermons Preached on Plantations to Congregations of Negroes* (1844; reprint ed., Freeport, N.Y.: Books for Libraries Press, 1971), pp. 89–95.

29. Leonard Lovett, "Perspective on the Black Origins of the Contemporary Pentecostal Movement," a paper delivered before the Society for the Study of Black Religion, New York City, October 27, 1972, p. 19.

30. Rawick, *American Slave,* vol. 7, part 2, p. 121.

31. Ibid., vol. 3, part 3, p. 247.

32. Ibid., part 4, p. 63.

33. James Weldon Johnson, *God's Trombones* (New York: Viking Press, 1969), p. 21.

34. Rawick, *American Slave,* vol. 2, part 2, p. 35.

35. Roberts, *Liberation and Reconciliation,* p. 88.

36. Benjamin Drew, *The Refugee: A North-side View of Slavery* (1855; reprint ed., Reading, Mass.: Addison-Wesley, 1969), p. 35.

37. Sojourner Truth, *Narrative and Book of Life* (1875; reprint ed., Chicago: Johnson Publishing Co., 1970), pp. 40–41.

38. Truth, *Narrative and Book of Life,* p. 38.

39. Frederick Douglass, *My Bondage and My Freedom* (1855: reprint ed., New York: Arno Press, 1969), pp. 144–145.

40. Pennington, "Fugitive Blacksmith," p. 256.

41. Fisk University, "Unwritten History," p. 48.

42. Galatians 6:9.

43. Rawick, *American Slave,* vol. 7, part 1, p. 219.

44. Ibid., vol. 3, part 3, p. 260.

45. Fisk University, "Unwritten History," p. 167.

46. Ibid., p. 166.

47. Craft, "Running a Thousand Miles," p. 275.

48. Herbert Aptheker, *Nat Turner's Slave Rebellion* (New York: Grove Press, 1968), p. 38.

49. Pennington, "Fugitive Blacksmith," p. 262.

50. Drew, *Refugee,* p. 236.

51. Fisk University, "Unwritten History," p. 30.

52. Rawick, *American Slave,* vol. 7, part 2, p. 113.

53. Ibid., vol. 5, part 4, p. 240.

54. Ibid., vol. 2, part 2, pp. 53–54.

55. William R. Jones, *Is God a White Racist?: A Preamble to Black Theology* (Garden City, N.Y.: Doubleday Anchor, 1973), pp. xix–xxi.

56. Fisk University, "Unwritten History," p. 189.

57. Ibid., pp. 284–291.

58. Rawick, *American Slave,* vol. 1, part 1, p. 234.

59. Jones, *God a White Racist?,* pp. 1–23.

60. Ibid., pp. 185–202.

61. Charles Albert Tindley, "We'll Understand It Better By and By," *Gospel Pearls* (Nashville: Sunday School Publishing Board, National Baptist Convention, 1921), p. 107.

5. American Black Folk Beliefs

1. Rattray, *Ashanti Proverbs*, p. 25.

2. Delano, *Yoruba Proverbs*, p. 87.

3. Fisk University, "Unwritten History," pp. 210–211.

4. Ibid., pp. 191, 195, 197.

5. Rawick, *American Slave*, vol. 7, part 2, p. 48.

6. Quoted in Leslie Fishell, Jr., and Benjamin Quarles, *The Negro American: A Documentary History* (Glenview, Ill.: Scott Foresman, 1967), pp. 135–136.

7. Josiah Henson, *An Autobiography of the Reverend Josiah Henson* (1881; reprint ed. Reading Mass.: Addison Wesley, 1969), pp. 36–37. The commonly raised questions regarding the historical authenticity of this narrative do not effect the value of this example of folk beliefs.

8. Rawick, *American Slave*, vol. 2, part 1, p. 106.

9. Ibid., vol. 3, part 4, pp. 178–179.

10. Henson, *Autobiography*, p. 83.

11. Ibid.

12. Ibid., p. 84.

13. Vassa, "Life of Gustavus Vassa," p. 4.

14. Ibid., p. 35.

15. Ibid., p. 114.

16. Rawick, *American Slave*, vol. 6, part 1, p. 301.

17. Ibid., vol. 3, part 4, p. 173.

18. Rom. 8:28 (author's translation).

19. Walker, *Spirit Possession*, p. 140.

20. Fisk University, "Unwritten History," p. 224. Cf. John 3:8.

21. Rawick, *American Slave*, vol. 7, part 1, p. 205.

22. Bastide, *African Civilisations*, pp. 5–12.

23. See p. 11.

24. Higginson, *Army Life in a Black Regiment*, p. 17.

25. Walker, *Spirit Possession*, pp. 72–73.

26. Rawick, *American Slave*, vol. 5, part 3, p. 33.

27. Ibid., vol. 4, part 1, p. 85.

28. Ibid., vol. 6, part 1, p. 316.

29. Ibid., vol. 2, part 2, p. 87.

30. Ibid., vol. 5, part 3, p. 179.

31. Walker, *Spirit Possession*, p. 6.

32. Ibid., p. 86.
33. Ibid., p. 33.
34. Ibid., p. 2.
35. Ibid., p. 34.
36. Ibid., p. 83.
37. Ibid., p. 84.
38. Ibid., p. 130.
39. Gal. 5:22.

Bibliography

Books

Anderson, Jourdan. "To My Old Master," in Frances S. Freedman, ed. *The Black Experience.* New York: Bantam Books, 1970.

Aptheker, Herbert. *Nat Turner's Slave Rebellion.* New York: Grove Press, 1968.

Bastide, Roger. *African Civilisations in the New World.* New York: Harper & Row, 1971.

Beattie, John, and Middleton, John. *Spirit Mediumship and Society in Africa.* New York: Africana, 1969.

Blassingame, John W. *The Slave Community.* New York: Oxford University Press, 1972.

Borneman, Ernest. "The Roots of Jazz," in Nat Hentoff and A. J. McCarthy, eds. *Jazz.* New York: Rinehart, 1959.

Burton, Richard F. *Wit and Wisdom from West Africa* in the series *Afro-American Studies.* New York: New American Library, 1969 (original publication 1865).

Busia, K. A. "Ashanti," in Daryll Forde, ed. *African Worlds.* London: Oxford University Press, 1954.

Christensen, James Boyd. "The Adaptive Functions of Fanti Priesthood," in W. R. Bacom and M. J. Herskovits, eds. *Continuity and Change in African Cultures.* Chicago: University of Chicago Press, 1959.

Cobbs, Price M., and Grier, William H. *The Jesus Bag.* New York: McGraw-Hill, 1971.

Craft, William. "Running a Thousand Miles for Freedom," in Arna Bontemps, ed. *Great Slave Narratives*. Boston: Beacon Press, 1969.

Danquah, J. B. *The Akan Doctrine of God*. London: Frank Cass & Co., 1968.

Delano, Isaac O. *Owe L'Esin Oro: Yoruba Proverbs—Their Meaning and Usage*. Ibadan, Nigeria: Oxford University Press, 1966.

Douglass, Frederick. *My Bondage and My Freedom*. New York: Arno Press, 1969 (original publication 1855).

———. *Narrative of the Life and Times of Frederick Douglass, An American Slave,* edited by Benjamin Quarles. Cambridge: Harvard University Press, 1960.

Drew, Benjamin. *The Refugee: A North-side View of Slavery*. Reading, MA: Addison-Wesley, 1969 (original publication 1855).

DuBois, W. E. B. *The Negro*. New York: Oxford University Press, 1970.

Ezeanya, Stephan N. "God, Spirits and the Spirit World," in Kwesi A. Dickson and Paul Ellingworth, eds. *Biblical Revelation and African Beliefs*. Maryknoll, NY: Orbis Books, 1969.

Finnegan, Ruth. *Oral Literature in Africa*. Oxford: Clarendon Press, 1970.

Fishel, Leslie H., Jr., and Quarles, Benjamin. *The Negro American: A Documentary History*. Glenview, IL: Scott, Foresman and Company, 1967.

Frazier, E. Franklin. *The Negro Church in America*. New York: Schocken Books, 1963.

Genovese, Eugene D. *Roll, Jordan, Roll*. N.Y.: Pantheon Books, 1974.

Glennie, Alexander. *Sermons Preached on Plantations to Congregations of Negroes*. Freeport, NY: Books for Libraries Press, 1971 (original publication 1844).

Goldenson, Robert M. *Encyclopedia of Human Behaviour*. Garden City, NY: Doubleday & Co., 1970.

Grimal, Pierre, ed. *Larousse World Mythology*. Translated by Patricia Beardsworth. New York: G. P. Putnam's Sons, 1965.

Harding, Vincent. "Preface to the Atheneum Edition," in Benjamin E. Mays (ed.) *The Negro's God*. New York: Atheneum, 1969 (original publication 1938).

Henson, Josiah. *An Autobiography of the Reverend Josiah Henson*. Reading, MA: Addison-Wesley, 1969 (original publication 1881).

Herskovits, Melville J. *The Myth of the Negro Past*. Boston: Beacon Press, 1941.

Higginson, Thomas Wentworth. *Army Life in a Black Regiment.* Boston: Beacon Press, 1962 (original publication 1869).

Idowu, E. Bolaji. "Introduction," in Kwesi A. Dickson and Paul Ellingworth, eds. *Biblical Revelation and African Beliefs.* Maryknoll, NY: Orbis Books, 1969.

_____. *Olodumare God in Yoruba Belief.* London: Longman Group Limited, 1962.

Johnson, James Weldon. *God's Trombones.* New York: Viking Press, 1969.

Jones, LeRoi. *Blues People.* New York: William Morrow and Company, 1963.

Jones, William R. *Is God a White Racist?* Garden City, N.Y.: Doubleday Anchor, 1973.

Jung, Carl G. *Psychology and Religion.* New Haven: Yale University Press, 1938.

Kponkpogori, C. S., Natomaj, C. J., and Rytz, O. *Gonja Proverbs,* edited by O. Rytz. Local Studies Series, No. 3. Legon, Ghana: Institute of African Studies, 1966.

Lester, Julius. *The Seventh Son.* New York: Random House, 1971.

Lucas, J. Olumide. *The Religion of the Yorubas.* Lagos, Nigeria: C. M. S. Bookshop, 1948.

Mbiti, John S. *African Religions and Philosophy.* New York: Praeger, 1969.

_____. *Concepts of God in Africa.* New York: Praeger, 1970.

Mercier, P. "The Fon of Dahomey," in Daryll Forde, ed. *African Worlds.* London: Oxford University Press, 1954.

Parrinder, Geoffrey. *African Mythology.* London: Paul Hamlyn, 1967.

Pennington, J. W. C. "The Fugitive Blacksmith," in Arna Bontemps, ed. *Great Slave Narratives.* Boston: Beacon Press, 1969.

Plumpp, Sterling D. *Black Rituals.* Chicago: Third World Press, 1972.

Puckett, Newbell Niles. *The Magic and Folk Beliefs of the Southern Negro.* 2d ed. New York: Dover Publications, 1969.

Rattray, R. Sutherland. *Ashanti Proverbs.* Oxford: Clarendon Press, 1914.

Rawick, George P. *The American Slave:* A Composite Autobiography. 19 Vols. Westport, CT: Greenwich Publishing Company, 1972.

Roberts, J. Deotis. *Liberation and Reconciliation: A Black Theology.* Philadelphia: Westminster Press, 1971.

Rosenberg, Bruce A. *The Art of the American Folk Preacher.* New York: Oxford University Press, 1970.

Sannes, G. W. *African 'Primitives': Function and Form in African Masks and Figures,* translated by Margaret King. New York: Africana Publishing Corporation, 1970.

Smith, Charles Spencer. *A History of the African Methodist Episcopal Church.* Vol. 2. Philadelphia: Book Concern of the A.M.E. Church, 1922 (reprinted New York: Johnson Reprint Corporation, 1968).

Stack, Carol B. *All Our Kin: Strategies for Survival in a Black Community.* New York: Harper & Row, 1974.

Tindley, Charles Albert. "We'll Understand It Better By and By," in *Gospel Pearls.* Nashville: Sunday School Publishing Board, National Baptist Convention, U.S.A., Inc., 1921.

Truth, Sojourner. *Narrative and Book of Life.* Chicago: Johnson Publishing Co., 1970 (original publication 1875).

Vassa, Gustavus. "The Life of Gustavus Vassa, the African," in Arna Bontemps, ed. *Great Slave Narratives.* Boston: Beacon Press, 1969.

Walker, Sheila S. *Ceremonial Spirit Possession in Africa and Afro-America.* Leiden, Holland: E. J. Brill, 1972.

Washington, Joseph H., Jr. *Black Sects and Cults.* Garden City, NY: Doubleday & Co., 1972.

Webster's New International Dictionary. Springfield, MA: G & C Merriam Co., 1927.

Wilmore, Gayraud S. *Black Religion and Black Radicalism.* Garden City, NY: Doubleday & Co., 1972.

Woodson, Carter G. *The History of the Negro Church.* 3d ed. Washington, D.C.: Associated Publishers, 1972.

_____. *The African Background Outlined: Or, Handbook for the Study of the Negro.* Westport, Conn.: Negro Universities Press, 1973 (original publication, 1936).

Articles

Adesanya, Adebayo. "Yoruba Metaphysical Thinking." *Odu* Nos. 4–6 (1957–1958): 37.

Horton, Robin. "Conference: 'The High God in Africa.' " *Odu* II:2 (January 1966): 88.

Hudson, Winthrop S. "Shouting Methodists." *Encounter* XXIX:1 (Winter 1968): 73–84.

Jones, Lawrence N. "They Sought a City: The Black Church and Churchmen in the Nineteenth Century." *Union Seminary Quarterly Review* XXVI:258 (Spring 1971).

Mbiti, John S. "Christianity and Traditional Religions in Africa." *Inter-*

national Review of Mission, LIX:236 (October 1970): 435.

Patterson, Orlando. "Toward a Future That Has No Past—Reflections on the Fate of Blacks in the Americas." *The Public Interest,* XXVII (Spring 1972): 47, 61.

Rowell, Charles H. "An Interview with Alvin Aubert: The Black Poet in the Afternoon." *Black World,* XXII:10 (August 1973): 37.

Tavris, Carol. "Magic & Medicine, A Sketch of Thomas Lambo." *Psychology Today* (February 1972): 65.

Verger, Pierre. "The Yoruba High God." *Odu,* II:2 (January 1966): 38–41.

Other Sources

Fisk University Social Research Institute Slave Narratives Collection, 1929–30. Manuscript in my possession incomplete. Field data from Tennessee and Kentucky, compiled at Nashville, Tennessee.

Gotom, Musa. Anga doctoral candidate, Claremont, California.

Lovett, Leonard. "Perspective on the Black Origins of the Contemporary Pentecostal Movement." A paper delivered before the Society for the Study of Black Religion, New York City, October 27, 1972.

Index

75 76 77 78 79 10 9 8 7 6 5 4 3 2 1